D1276169

On Calderón

On Calderón

James E. Maraniss

University of Missouri Press
Columbia & London, 1978

Library of Congress Cataloging in Publication Data

Maraniss, James E   1945–
    On Calderón.

    Bibliography: p. 123
    Includes index.
    1.   Calderón de la Barca, Pedro, 1600–1681—Criticism
and interpretation.   I.   Title.
PQ6312.M3   862'.3   77–14034
ISBN 0–8262–0237–3

The translations appended to this book are my own. I
have attempted the usual unsatisfactory compromise
between fidelity and grace, and I think that the former, at
least, will be found in them.   J.E.M. 16 November 1977

Frontispiece is from *Monstrances* by Lucas Cranach,
Wittenberg, 1509; reprinted from Ernst Lehner, *Alphabets and
Ornaments* (New York and Cleveland: The World Publishing
Company, 1952).

To Stephen Gilman and Edmund L. King

Contents

On Calderón

1

Introduction

Calderón's theater is the sober celebration of order triumphant—a celebration of the order of the universe; of the state; of the family; of the human personality; and, not the least, of language and thought. His plays are conceived in the spirit of demonstration; they show the value and the vulnerability of the powers of restraint, discipline, and renunciation; and they solemnize, with a grim logic, the will and ingenuity necessary to keep life's chaotic impulses under control. Plays of this type, which include some of European literature's greatest dramatic works, would hardly have survived their own time if they did not in some ways transcend their didactic propositions with a personal vision of life as it is lived and dreamed and acted; yet they are still essentially demonstrations, and the actions they set forth result less from a direct observation of life than from the application of thought and feeling to a preexisting literary world, the world of the *comedia*. In reading Calderón one must keep the *comedia* of Lope de Vega in mind as a subtext, as a set of conventions and possibilities, of actions and implicit meanings, from which Calderón borrows and refashions verse forms, images, themes, characters, and even entire plots. Calderón is a remaker and rearranger as much as he is an inventor, yet his plays are unique and unmistakable; they have been made out of the *comedia*, but made to serve a new end: to serve order as an end in itself.

Anyone seeking to learn about Spanish life during the Golden Age should look at the plays of Lope de Vega. Lope "imitates" life, his own as often as not, and his imitations have in turn affected the actions and self-conceptions of his audience to such a degree that most modern notions of what "real life" was like for Lope and his contemporaries derive in some way from an intuitive response to Lope's plays themselves. But no matter how faithful the *comedia* of Lope may be to the life of the time, it is still a self-sufficient poetic world of action and movement—a created world. Calderón's world is a creation upon a creation, and for this reason alone it is a criticism both of Lope's created world and, at a greater distance, of Spanish life. Lope's genius is such that no subsequent playwright, not even the great craftsman Calderón, could improve upon Lope's initial creation. What Calderón does is bring his own sense of order and logic, his own peculiar obsessions, to Lope's literary world; and in so doing he transforms it into something quite different from, and in some ways antithetical to, Lope's theater. Although Calderón's theater is closer to Lope's *comedia* than to anything else, it is also cut off, unique, alone in a way that the theater of no other Spanish playwright is. Calderón's method of borrowing, because it serves his thought, results in plays that are distinct from his models.

To the hotly flowing theatrical language of Lope de Vega, Calderón brings coldly passionate discipline; his verses always scan, his grammar never fails, his images, no matter how extravagant, never get out of control. His best passages are triumphs of thought and schematization:

> de la pena mía
> no sé la naturaleza:
> que entonces fuera tristeza
> lo que hoy es melancolía.
> Solo sé que sé sentir;
> lo que sé sentir no sé;
> que ilusión del alma fue.†[1]

Yet this language, for all its coherence, can be violent, in the sense that its logical abstractness and total control inhibit lyric consummation and repose. His mind is always more subtle than his senses, and it enables him to lead his characters out of difficult situations; but still the irrational intrudes, and Calderón's logic can fence it in but cannot disarm it. His plots, so carefully and tightly worked out, envelop more ambiguities than do the loose precursors from which they are molded. Critics still argue over the essential meaning of some

---

† This symbol indicates that an English translation is given in the Appendix, pp. 106–22.

1. Pedro Calderón de la Barca, *El príncipe constante*, in *Obras completas*, 5th ed., vol. 1, ed. A. Valbuena Briones (Madrid: Aguilar, 1966), p. 250.

of Calderón's most limpidly syllogistic plays. It is not surprising that the last word about an elusive ironist such as Lope should never be written; but Calderón, who seems so straightforward in his none-too-subtle logic, should not have caused as much controversy as he has. That he has done so indicates that there is more in his plays than can be perfectly controlled, no matter how persistent the effort. It may not be possible to establish exactly what that "more" is. It could be the ghostly presence of the playwright's repressed emotions; or his resigned awareness that order and control demand a high, sometimes terrible, price; or inevitable resistance to the outside control inherent in life itself; or the expression of a contradiction in the seventeenth-century Spanish consciousness. All of these are plausible hypotheses and merit consideration.

It could be argued that Calderón's raw material, the *comedia* of Lope, does not offer the best opportunity for elaborating serious problems. Lope's plays have a way of skirting problems or subsuming them in lyricism; mostly, they deal uncritically (or rather, on many sympathetically conceived levels) with received values: national myths, heroism, affective religion, popular cultural motifs. Américo Castro has asserted, convincingly, that in Spain, by the seventeenth century, the Inquisition had done its work so well that the avoidance of critical thought had become the common practice. Cervantes, an uncommon writer by any standard, is not a *comedia* playwright for reasons that include an inability to accept the whole body of received dogmas and transcendent values associated with the ascendancy of the caste of *cristianos viejos*.[2] Nevertheless, Calderón's reshaping of the *comedia* does bring out, and seek solutions to, some problems, albeit not in a way that could be termed a systematic criticism of Spanish national values as they are embodied in the *comedia*; rather he heightens some of the *comedia*'s inherent contradictions. His obsession with the problem of order leads him to create a world on stage that alters and undercuts some of the *comedia*'s vital presuppositions and raises new problems that are more personal, less social, and, because of their logical abstractness, more susceptible to logical analysis.

2. See especially Américo Castro's introduction ("Por qué fue dualmente conflictiva la literatura del siglo XVI") to his *Hacia Cervantes*, pp. 10–25.

The *comedia* survives because of its adequacy in represent-
ing certain ways of being and acting that are interesting in
themselves and are made more so through the contributions of
several great dramatic poets. It is the theater of celebration,
not of analysis. Like the Hollywood movie industry, it has fed
the escapist aspirations of a mass audience. For every Hollywood cliché (the happy ending, the gangster who gets his just
reward, the noble sacrifice) one could find an analogous convention in the *comedia*, just as predictable and just as circum-
scribed by the narrow limits of public tolerance and taste. Both
Hollywood and the *comedia* have produced a great deal of trash
and ephemera, and both at times have received the second-
best efforts of some excellent writers who write down to their
audience with some flippancy and cynicism. Yet the *comedia*
playwrights and the Hollywood screenwriters and directors
succeed in giving an entire culture a picture of its real or imagined life in precise and poetic images that, however unso-
phisticated they may be in their subject matter, are sometimes
of great aesthetic power.

An ordinary Hollywood Western, in many ways comparable
to an ordinary *comedia* "honor play," might be built upon a
plot that goes something like this: a villain, or group of vil-
lains (outlaws or Indians), commits an atrocity upon a good,
innocent man's wife or family; the innocent man sets out in
search of the malefactors; eventually he catches up with them,
punishes them, and the moral balance is regained. During the
course of the film, the protagonist will have a series of adventures in which he will show courage, resourcefulness, determination, self-reliance, and other traits highly regarded by the
American public; the adventures are set in a mythic past and
are given concreteness through specific actions: taming a horse,
shooting the rapids, following a trail. Some of these events
occur in two very good, but very different, movies: *The Search-
ers* (John Ford, 1956) and *Rancho Notorious* (Fritz Lang, 1951).
The films use similar character types, they are set in the same
historical period, and their plots have much in common; yet
in their depictions of human experience these films do not resemble each other. Ford, through his visual composition, selec-
tion of events, timing, and direction of actors, underlines the
ceremonial bonds that bind men to a common enterprise; he
celebrates American values. Lang, a Central European with

preoccupations of his own, uses fatalistic camera angles to communicate determinism; and he directs scenes (such as the one in which Marlene Dietrich is a dance-hall girl riding on a drunken cowboy's back in a saloon race) so that they emphasize power relationships among men. When Ford's hero avenges himself, he is wise enough to see the futility of vengeance; Lang's hero becomes corrupted in the search for justice.

A history of the Hollywood Western that presumes to encompass the works of both Ford and Lang should make a distinction between the general characteristics of the genre, which appear in the works of both directors, and the personal stylistic traits that make their works unique. Such a distinction must be based upon a study of their means of expression, which are visual: camera angles, movements, pictorial compositions. From this study the critic might deduce each director's attitude toward the values implicit in the Western as well as each director's idea of significant human action. It is not possible to distinguish a Ford Western from a Lang Western without looking beyond what is on the surface, beyond the general characteristics common to all Hollywood Westerns. Likewise, a historian of the *comedia* must see beyond the obvious similarities between an honor play by Lope and one by Calderón to find the personal stylistic traits of each, which in turn carry visions of life that can be independent of the meanings implicitly conveyed by the honor play as a generic entity. The honor play is the common property of a whole society; at the same time, each particular play by Lope or by Calderón is an individual perception and re-creation of the world and cannot be treated simply as a manifestation of the society, although it certainly is that, too.

Américo Castro, in his discussions of the social basis of the Spanish honor drama, is careful to point out that social conditions cannot be said to have caused the appearance of such works as *Peribáñez* or *El alcalde de Zalamea*; they can only be said to have made these plays possible.[3] Historical criticism,

3. "Tan altas expresiones poéticas reposaban, desde luego, sobre situaciones españoles muy agudizadas desde el siglo XV, aunque sin conexión causativa con la grandeza de figuras como Peribáñez o Pedro Crespo." ("Such high poetic expressions rested, of course, upon Spanish circumstances that had been severely straitened since the fifteenth century, al-

especially of the kind and quality practiced by Castro, can be especially helpful in forcing the distinction between the general and the unique. If one accepts (and there is no good reason not to) Castro's contention that in the Spain of Calderón's time direct critical treatment of society's obsession with honor was, because of its caste basis, scarcely possible in an art dependent upon acceptance by a mass audience, he can more easily focus attention upon aspects of Calderón's plays not directly connected with the honor plot. The honor plot is there, but what happens within the honor plot and the ends to which Calderón bends the plot are of greater interest than the plot itself. Preoccupation with honor, however strange it may seem now, is certainly taken for granted as a fact of life by the *comedia* playwrights. This intuition of Castro's can be backed up sufficiently to convince the skeptical, if not the hostile (whose writings will be given some attention herein).

Castro, in his later writings, has come to reject his own earlier studies of honor as a static idea and to view it as a historical process, an activity. It should be apparent that in the *comedia*, too, honor is an activity; it informs a series of stage actions that, as Castro has argued, seem to be analogous to certain historical actions. Viewed in the abstract, independent of the particular handling of a given playwright, the honor activity, which is probably the single most common and characteristic feature of all seventeenth-century Spanish plays, has an outline that to the modern reader is as fearsome as it is predictable. In the honor plays, the honor activity involves a response to a threat to the protagonist's reputation, brought about by the real or suspected infidelity of his wife, daughter, sister, or other female relative, which provokes a terrible effort to keep the "dishonor" secret, usually through the elimination of the offending parties. There are other types of plays in the *comedia* that have plots dealing with the protection of honor and reputation: the so-called cape-and-sword play, in which honor is preserved not through vengeance but through marriage, and the peasant honor drama, in which a peasant-hero assumes the role of a man of honor to protect a reputation

---

though these circumstances could not be called causative of the greatness of such figures as Peribáñez or Pedro Crespo.") Américo Castro, *De la edad conflictiva*, p. 66.

threatened by a nobleman's misbehavior. A sense of personal honor informs the motives of all *comedia* characters (with the occasional but not automatic exception of the *graciosos*). In historical plays, such as Lope's *Pedro Carbonero* or Calderón's *El príncipe constante*, the national honor of Spain and the honor of Catholicism, both as an institution and as a set of beliefs, are upheld and affirmed. There are plays such as Calderón's *La vida es sueño*, in which the honor plot serves as a subplot, almost as a key to understanding the main plot. Calderón even includes the honor action in some of his *autos sacramentales*; in the *auto* titled *El pintor de su deshonra*, God himself is the dishonored party.

The plot of a *comedia* honor play, like the plot of a Hollywood Western, can be understood in terms of social values in action. Castro, taking as his point of departure a recognition of the strangeness of such plays as *Peribáñez*—in which a peasant acts to defend his honor in a way usually associated with the class values of the nobility—has come to regard the honor values not as ones of class but as ones of caste. According to Castro, Lope's Peribáñez and Calderón's Pedro Crespo are the idealized incarnations of the pure caste of *cristianas viejos*, untainted by Moorish or Jewish blood. "Limpio linaje" is a character's proof of title in the *comedia*; and this concept can be expressly stated, as it is by Pedro Crespo:

> Dime, por tu vida, ¿o hay alguien
> que no sepa que yo soy,
> si bien de limpio linaje,
> hombre llano?†[4]

Where it is not expressly stated, it is implied in the working out of the honor plot, where so much of what a character is depends upon what others think he is. As Spanish society through the Inquisition sacrificed a part of its own body to eliminate the source of racial and ideological impurity, so the heroes of the honor plays carry out their purges against the sources of their dishonor:

> En esa misma sociedad en donde las personas—solas,
> quietas en cuanto crear objetos materiales o mentales—se

4. Pedro Calderón de la Barca, *El alcalde de Zalamea*, in *Obras completas*, 1:545.

enfrentaban con el monstruo de la opinión, en ese ambiente,
urgía mostrarse "hombre," mantener hombría frente a la
mujer amada como presa codiciable, cuyo amor puede
tornarse nube frágil y huidiza. Toda faceta humana expuesta
a las ráfagas de la opinión, se volvió tema dramático capaz de
encandilar el ánimo y la fantasía del público de los corrales.[5]

It is not difficult to accept that it is this analogy between
honor and caste that moves Lope to Vega to use the honor plot
so often. Honor plays are crowd pleasers, as Lope himself says
in his ironic apologia, *Arte nuevo*:

> Los casos de la honra son mejores
> porque mueven con fuerza a toda gente
> (Matters of honor are the best,
> for they move everyone, and strongly)

One may deplore the taste of Lope's audience, just as one may
deplore the taste of an American movie audience. One may regard the social values enacted in an honor play as brutal and
unreflective, responsible for an inhuman ritual of sacrifice in
the service of an immoral social code (the consequences of this
social code for Spanish civilization are now well known, and
Castro has devoted his life's work to an attempt at alleviating
the consequences through understanding and self-analysis of
the most generous and encompassing kind). One might regret
some of the obvious limitations of the honor plot, most of all
its inability to convey a truly tragic sense of life, an inability
due largely to the playwrights' insufficient provision for a realization by the sacrificer (the husband, and the man of honor)
that he himself has been partly responsible for the existence of
the sacrificed—that is, there is a lack of "tragic realization."
Almost all recent critics and scholars who have dealt with the
comedia have expressed various degrees of shock and dismay

5. "In that same society in which men—alone, their desires and capac-
ities for the creation of physical and intellectual objects rendered quies-
cent—had to encounter the monster of public opinion, in that ambience,
one had to show oneself to be a 'man,' to maintain one's maleness before
the woman loved as an enviable possession, whose love could become a
frail and fleeting cloud. Every human trait exposed to the blasts of public
opinion was converted into a dramatic theme capable of inflaming the
souls and fantasies of the public in the theaters." Castro, *De la edad
conflictiva*, p. 211.

at the implied values of the honor play and at the state of the society from which they come. Often, especially in the case of recent Calderonian critics in England, some sort of critical attempt, usually unconvincing, is made to force a separation between the playwright and the honor ideology, even to the extent of maintaining that the playwright is consciously condemning that ideology.

Impossible as it may be to divorce the meanings of the generic honor plot from the concrete meanings of individual plays, we need not reduce our reaction to those plays to an appalled rejection of the honor values or assume that *comedia* writers, whose works are so admirable in other respects, must also doubt those values. Lope uses the honor plot, as Ford and Lang use the Western plot, as a frame (one sure to be a popular success) to enable him to present certain states of being and acting that are closer to his expressive purpose and poetic sensibility than are the honor values. Lope is an erotic poet, a writer who seems to take nothing seriously, except for art and love in all its forms. In his honor plays, of whatever kind, Lope elaborates the poetry of spontaneous affection, of passion and loss, of jealousy, deceit, grace and courtship, love of country, of God, unifying Platonic love, impersonally beautiful sexual aggression—almost any amorous state or love-caused way of behaving imaginable—and he always does so with a multileveled ironic delicacy and poetic grace. Eros is the great uniter in Lope's plays; it erases contradictions and links enemies. In *Peribáñez*, the Comendador's love for Casilda complements and even assists the perfect union of man and wife; the Comendador dies for love as beautifully as Peribáñez and Casilda live for it.

In the theater of Calderón, honor plots similar to those found in Lope's plays are used toward different ends: to enact conflicts between the forces of disruption and a desire for control. In such a context Eros becomes a problem in itself and is no longer available as a means of nullifying or transcending other problems. The amorous actions and situations that Calderón's plays might share with the *comedias* of Lope acquire a darker meaning; love appears as an impure thought or an attempted rape, as an evil woman or a melancholy distraction, as an illusion, as a source of sadness, deceit, and, most of all, disorder. Calderón's lovers triumph through a renunciation of their

love (Segismundo renounces Rosaura, Cipriano and Justina
find union only in martyrdom); and when they are united in
marriage, as in *La dama duende,* the marriage comes as a truce.
Eros in Calderón has a quickness and glitter, a flashy surface,
as in the love chorus of *El mágico prodigioso*:

> Una Voz: ¿Cuál es la gloria mayor
> de esta vida?
> Coro: Amor, amor.
> Una Voz: No hay sujeto en quien no imprima
> el fuego de amor su llama,
> pues vive más donde ama
> el hombre, que a donde anima.
> Amor solamente estima
> cuanto tener vida sabe
> el tronco, la flor y el ave;
> luego es la gloria mayor
> de esta vida . . .
> Coro: Amor, amor.†[6]

This chorus is led by the Devil, to tempt Justina away from
the true path of renunciation and martyrdom. Such a scene
might occur in a play by Lope; but the chorus would more
probably be a chorus of shepherds, and the mood would be
authentically celebrative. In *El mágico prodigioso,* the scene has
an undertone of futility and danger. The titles of Calderón's
plays alone tell what he thinks of pleasure: *No hay más fortuna
que Dios, La vida es sueño, Las cadenas del demonio.* Calderón states explicitly, and demonstrates (by using the forms
of the *comedia,* which are most typically, at least with Lope, an
incarnation of the most transcendental values in the most human of actions) the gulf between this world and the next, the
futility of earthly action, and the advisability of cleaving unto
the eternal. In those plays in which a strictly terrestrial plane
of action inhibits any explicit contrast between the rewards of
this world and those of the next (the honor plays and the cape-
and-sword plays), Calderón creates a feeling of melancholy
hopelessness and self-negating theatricality. Even as Calderón
demonstrates, with the greatest sympathy, the need to main-

6. Pedro Calderón de la Barca, *El mágico prodigioso,* in *Obras completas,* 1:632.

tain order by protecting the ideal of honor, he shows that the process, because of the terrible price and the need for dissimulation and trickery it entails, is a difficult and pathetic, if not a tragic, one.

A conflict between rash impulse and controlling reaction characterizes all of Calderón's plays, giving them a fundamental duality of action that sets them apart from Lope's unifying dramas of love. Calderón's dualities can be formulated in sharp intellectual terms: love versus honor, freedom versus restraint, earthly pleasure versus divine glory, personal interest versus national interest, belief in life versus belief in afterlife, rebellion versus containment. These dualities, which Lope transcends or avoids, are the problems of Calderón's theater; it is in the treatment of these issues that he shows his intellect and his strange passion, which is, as Calderón himself might describe it, both icy and inflamed.

Calderón's intellect must be taken for what it is in order to be appreciated rightly. His contemporaries fittingly designated him the "Monstruo del Ingenio," a title that both sets him apart from Lope, the "Monstruo de la Naturaleza," and gives him the proper credit for his great gifts—his cleverness, the lucidity of his writing, his powers of association and contrast, his ability to pull off *coups de théâtre*. These qualities do not necessarily make an original thinker, much less a "philosophic" one. It was the German romantics—Goethe, Schlegel, and Tieck, the last two of whom translated Calderón into German —who elevated Calderón to the position of great philosopher, of a writer who not only posed life's important questions in his plays but went on to solve them. For this, the Schlegels thought Calderón superior to Shakespeare. Perhaps the Germans' admiration and overestimation of Calderón could be attributed to their joy in "discovering" a literature of which they had previously been unaware and which seemed to offer so much when compared to the classicism that was their immediate heritage. Perhaps they were attracted to Calderón's almost Germanic penchant for metaphysical abstraction and grand conception. The Schlegels most certainly liked Calderón's spiritualism and his Catholicism. But surely they were wrong about his originality; his answers are not new, they are old, and his theater forces a reimposition of medieval values upon a world that had already passed them by. This forced reimposition has its stylistic parallel in Calderón's schematization of Lope's freely flowing forms.

One can admire Calderón's mind without concluding that it is deeper than Lope's heart; it is not. Nor is Calderón's theater more mature than Lope's in its means of expressing human life in action, rather Calderón's fancy is bred not in the heart but in the head. Some of Calderón's early admirers among the romantics saw the difference soon enough; and as the nineteenth century advanced, Calderón's reputation declined. Shelley stated his disillusionment in his *Defence of Poetry*:

> Calderón . . . has attempted to fulfill some of the high conditions of dramatic representation neglected by Shakespeare; such as the establishing a relation between the drama and religion, and the accommodation of them to music and dancing; but he omits the observation of conditions still more important, and more is lost than gained by the substitution of the rigidly defined and ever-repeated idealisms of a distorted superstition for the living impersonations of the truth of human passion.[7]

This criticism, an overreaction to a previous overestimation, was soon taken up in England by the essayist and critic G. H. Lewes, who subverted Calderón's reputation as a thinker in the English-speaking world,[8] although it has been revived recently. In Spain it was taken up by Menéndez Pelayo, who could not forgive what he saw to be the immorality and tediousness of the honor plot and who scornfully dismissed Calderón's metaphysical reasonings as "ergotismo."[9] These attacks are not wholly deserved, and those who made them were perhaps seeking more from literature than one can reasonably expect to be given. It is idle to hold Calderón to a philosophical standard to which he does not aspire, nor should he be held responsible for the limitations of the honor plot. His metaphysical reasonings, as constrained as they may be by their orthodox axioms, can only reasonably be asked to meet a purely dramatic standard, which they do: in Calderón's theater ratiocination can be a kind of action, with its own dramatic meaning and merit. No

7. Percy Bysshe Shelley, *A Defence of Poetry,* in *Shelley's Critical Prose,* ed. Bruce R. McElderry, Jr. (Lincoln: University of Nebraska Press, 1967), p. 15.

8. George Henry Lewes, *Spanish Drama: Lope de Vega and Calderón.*

9. Marcelino Menéndez y Pelayo, *Calderón y su teatro.*

doubt Calderón's reasonings are meant to be convincing intellectually as well as dramatically, but the modern reader finds it difficult to share the belief that might make them so.

The ideological and moral positions that are axiomatic in Calderón's theater, though they can be illustrated and made vivid and compelling, cannot be proved; they are matters of faith. Lope de Vega may or may not have cared deeply about the subtleties of Catholic thought, the need to mantain honor, the greatness of the Spanish realm—principles that Castro has described as being, to the seventeenth-century Spaniard, "imposibles de analizar a fondo, y mucho menos de derrocar."[10] Lope takes these principles for granted and does not present them in his theater as problematic. But to Calderón they need defence, and he defends them in a manner that can justly be called reactionary; that is, he upholds the authority of husband, church, and state as necessary for the maintenance of the order that is his obsession. His desire to defend these principles affects his presentation of the threat to them. Because Calderón takes both the threat and the need for a defense so seriously, he has suffered the scorn and neglect of those who consider themselves progressive thinkers. Castro himself has been guilty of taking this attitude.

Fundamental to Calderón's theater is the idea that freedom can be defined in the vocabulary of restraint. This idea depends upon the belief that man is rational and capable of making reasonable choices. The choices made and celebrated in Calderón's theater, although they are free and logical within their setting, always lead to an affirmation of the orthodox values in which Calderón believes, even though they may not be values with which the modern reader can agree. In Calderón's theater it is rational to overcome one's animal instincts, to sacrifice earthly happiness to achieve salvation, to subordinate one's self-interest to the interests of church and state. Calderón is straightforward in his presentation of choices; in *La vida es sueño*, the prince must recognize and renounce his natural instincts in order to embrace his function as a leader of the state, as a restorer of the old regime that he himself has threatened. In Calderón's *autos sacramentales*, the allegorical figures who symbolize humanity make logical choices in favor of sal-

10. "Impossible to analyze in depth, let alone overthrow." Castro, *De la edad conflictiva*, p. 233.

vation; those who choose wrongly are damned. Calderón's liking for allegory is related to his ability to see all human beings as sharing certain circumstances that are essentially the same; one may find the kinds of choices and opportunities for renunciation most characteristic of the *autos* even in those plays that seem most similar, in their general outlines, to the *comedias* of Lope de Vega.

Calderón's affirmation of the act of choice usually makes his dramatic vision something other than a tragic one, no matter how melancholy his plays might be in their overall effect. The concept of freedom of choice appears in its clearest form in the *autos sacramentales*, sometimes even as an independent allegorical character such as *Libre Albedrío*; in the "metaphysical" plays, such as *El príncipe constante* and *La vida es sueño*, it is discussed openly and acted upon (Segismundo chooses restraint, Fernando chooses martyrdom); and in the honor plays it is implied. In Calderón's plays a correct choice brings peace, even salvation. Earthly appetites, and the strong emotions they arouse, are presented as a kind of limitation to Calderón's characters' efforts to achieve self-fulfillment. But these limitations can be overcome through acts of will; and Calderón constructs his plays to emphasize the will, which, no matter how powerful the obstacles to its functioning, always functions and always succeeds. The will triumphs with the aid of an explicit or implied heavenly intervention or sanction; and it can secure a heavenly reward compared with which most earthly glories are insignificant, although there are some earthly institutions, such as the Church, the family, and the state, that are elevated to the position of divinely protected gifts in themselves. Calderón's firm belief in these rewards keeps him (except, perhaps, in *El príncipe constante*) from being a real tragedian. Writers of tragedy show nothing like Calderón's faith in the power of will to overcome limitation. The Oedipus of Sophocles' drama, a strong and highly principled character, cannot escape the limitation inherent in his fate; in the tragedies of Racine and Shakespeare man's will is not represented as omnipotent, but rather as something like a fault of character for which man must pay a catastrophic price, even if he achieves his ends. Writers of tragedy underline limitation as a fact of life by writing plays in which the human will, as dramatized in actions plausibly possible in human terms, is kept distinct from the finally mysterious and adverse workings of the universe. No such distinction is made by Calderón. In Calderón's theater the correct courses of action are available to the characters; the plays are arranged to relate means to ends, and one must always assume that the ends justify the means. One might feel after reading one of Calderón's plays that no ends could justify the means invoked, but care must be taken to separate this impression from the play's own testimony, which is marshaled in such a way as to demonstrate the correct course of action. There are ambiguities, however, and the plays by Calderón that offer the most ambiguity are the honor plays, in which the means taken to maintain honor are so self-destructive that one finds it hard to believe that Calderón could retain faith in them, although there can be no doubt about his acceptance of the ends, which represent none other than the stability, however tenuous, that repression of the passions insures.

A theatrical, confused, quickened, and dreamlike life is to be found in all of Calderón's plays, not just those, such as *La vida es sueño*, that explicitly bring home the message that life is an illusion. The honor plays (whose plots, in the hands of other *comedia* playwrights, are elaborated with a relaxed certainty and comparatively little exaggeration) are charged with contradictions and self-defeating paradoxes, poetically heightened and violent to a degree that makes them seem to undermine the bases of all action. Calderón's brilliant linguistic associations can destroy or distort one's sense of reality. There is little that is lifelike in his characters' speech; its effect is to promote the belief that life itself is not lifelike, that reality must be sought elsewhere, in another world. This cannot be explained away by demonstrating that Calderón's theater is "theatrical" because it is built upon literature rather than upon life (though this is true), nor is it enough to say that all art is illusion built upon illusion. Calderón's theater enacts a kind of illusory life because Calderón himself assumes, and in this he is not alone among baroque writers, that life itself is an illusion. Beneath the glittering panoply of theatrical effects can be perceived the heart of an ascetic. To say that life is a dream is to say that all the world is a stage, an assertion that Shakespeare reserved for the melancholy stoic, Jacques.

Calderón's despair about this world does not extend to the next; his theater enhances the glory of God. His devaluation

of earthly life assists the spectator's vital and logical apprehension of the rewards of the life of the spirit. Calderón argues
for the spiritual life with all his logic; he illustrates his theological points with the resources available to him as a playwright,
and he reduces the pursuit of pleasure, through theatrical
distortion, so that it appears meaningless. For all the grimness
of his solutions to the problems of honor and statecraft, they
are meant to be seen as preferable to the alternative, anarchy.

Still, one might ask, is not all this a betrayal of the *comedia*?
Is not the *comedia*'s chief glory its heightening of the grace
and meaning of human action and love? Is not the theater that
Lope created a theater of light irony and spontaneity that, no
matter how disorganized, redeems itself and the life it enacts
through lyric affirmation? To these objections one might respond that the plays of Lope and Calderón have less in common than is generally supposed and that one's inevitable liking
for Lope need not prohibit an admiration for Calderón, though
he is difficult to love. Calderón is no lyricist, nor is he an ironist.
His justice is stern; he finds division where Lope finds unity;
he does not indulge his enemies; he does not believe in the redeeming power of love. But his very disbelief in erotic and
lyrical unification and reconciliation, which makes him so
different from Lope, gives his plays a certain kind of intensity
not found in those by Lope. Where conflicts can be seen but
not resolved, they drive on to inevitable conclusions with all
their excitement and contradictions intact. Many of Calderón's
plays are expressive of those states of mind that most acutely
need lyric resolution but cannot find it; hence, those states of
mind lead to actions that for all their (relative) rightness cannot remain pure. At the end of *El médico de su honra,* an audience (at least, a seventeenth-century audience) might have felt
the need for Gutierre to kill his wife to protect his honor and
integrity; still, the cost as shown by Calderón himself is very
high. At the end of *El alcalde de Zalamea,* Calderón seems to
assert that Crespo is dignified and ingenious, but perhaps also
that he is too crafty; in *La dama duende* the heroine gets mar-
ried, but she is still volatile and possibly dangerous. If Calderón's were a lyric drama it might find ways to give a real
sense of renewal or restoration, but it is not and does not.

This study will deal specifically with seven of Calderón's
plays: two *autos, Los encantos de la Culpa* and *El gran teatro*

del mundo; the "metaphysical" play *La vida es sueño*; the historico-religious play *El príncipe constante*; the peasant honor drama *El alcalde de Zalamea*; the drama of intrigue *La dama duende*; the honor drama *El médico de su honra*; and the *opéra comique, Eco y Narciso*. These are some of Calderón's very best works, and each typifies one of the major groupings into which all of his plays can be placed.

The plays to be studied have much in common. All partake of the outward apparatus of the *comedia*: reliance upon poetry to supply background; use of different verse forms for different, strongly typed situations; conventional endings; and conventional plots, usually having something to do with honor. *El médico de su honra* has a pure *comedia* honor plot; in *El alcalde de Zalamea* there is a rural honor plot of the *Peribáñez* type; *La dama duende* has a *comedia* cape-and-sword honor plot; *El príncipe constante* deals with national and religious honor; *La vida es sueño* has a *comedia* honor plot as a subplot. These plots alone show the extent to which Calderón's theater is built upon previous literature. In order to see most clearly the personal traits that set Calderón apart, his plays will be compared in some detail with certain of Lope de Vega's better-known plays.

But Calderón's plays differ from one another, too, most importantly in what Kenneth Burke would call their "circumferences," or backgrounds. The circumference of the *autos* includes both the world and the superworld; in the "metaphysical" plays it comprises an imaginary kingdom of the mind; in the historico-religious plays it is a mythic past; and in the cape-and-sword plays and the honor plays, it is the restricted world of seventeenth-century society. In general it may be said that the smaller the circumference, the more pessimistic and contradictory the play. In the plays with backgrounds that are social and contemporary, it is more difficult for Calderón's characters to find ways out of their complicated predicaments; and, whether Calderón sees it that way or not, the conflicts that are successfully, if fancifully, resolved in the *autos* must, in the honor plays, be faced from within, and in their resolution there is a distortion of the world.

2

Autos Sacramentales

Los encantos de la Culpa,[1] one of the best of Calderón's *autos sacramentales,* might be used to support Shelley's assertion that Calderón substitutes "the rigid idealisms of an outworn superstition for the truth of human passion."[2] If one does not restrict the "human" or the "true" to the plausible, Shelley's objection can be met. Surely this play is passionate, and much of its beauty derives from its grace in handling states of the soul that are all the purer for their freedom from the constraints of plausibly human conduct.

The characters, all fully allegorical, include an everyman figure, called simply el Hombre (or, for the purpose of the anecdote, *el cristiano Ulises*); his emotional and psychic qualities such as los cinco Sentidos and el Entendimiento, which are objectified into agents; and certain theological abstractions, for example, la Penitencia. The characters meet on a theatrical plane that is both human and divine, where the human cedes some of its inalienability and concreteness and the divine cedes some of its distance and mystery. The plot is original in its organization; although, like most of Calderón's plots, it relies upon a borrowed story—in this instance upon the story of Odysseus and Circe in Homer's *Odyssey* and, more immediately, upon the plot of one of Calderón' s earlier plays, *El mayor encanto, amor.* The story of *Los encantos de la Culpa* is a simple one, which can be summarized as follows:

El Hombre (in the allegorical role of Ulysses) is voyaging on his ship (the ship of life) with his Entendimiento and his five senses (which Calderón portrays as volatile and untrustwor-

1. Pedro Calderón de la Barca, *Los encantos de la Culpa,* in *Obras completas,* 5th ed., vol. 3, ed. A. Valbuena Prat (Madrid: Aguilar, 1952), p. 405.

2. Percy Bysshe Shelley, *A Defence of Poetry,* in *Shelley's Critical Prose,* ed. Bruce R. McElderry, Jr. (Lincoln: University of Nebraska Press, 1967), p. 15.

thy). Entendimiento, the pilot, leads the ship to a safe port; but el Hombre quickly shows his ingratitude by sending his senses out to look for pleasure, after having heard both sides of an argument between the senses and Entendimiento. The lines of the argument are clearly drawn:

> Entendimiento: ¡Que como Humanos Sentidos
> todos deseado habéis
> hallar cada uno el objeto
> que más conviene a su ser!
> ¿No fuera mejor que fuera
> la tosca Tebaída, en quien
> la penitencia se hallara
> riyéndose del poder
> de las cortes populosas
> puesto que tan cierto es
> que sin pena de esta vida
> no hay en la eterna placer?
>
> Hombre: ¡Y que como Entendimiento
> has hablado tú! ¡Que estés
> siempre aconsejando penas
> a mis Sentidos! ¿No ves
> que son Sentidos humanos
> y que al fin es menester
> alivios que los diviertan
> de las fatigas en que
> han nacido?†[3]

The senses go forth to seek delight, which they find in the company of la Culpa (a Circe figure) and her retinue, the seven deadly sins. (All of the sins are feminine characters; this is perhaps due to the accident of the Spanish language or the design of the Christian tradition, but it suits Calderón's thought well enough.) Soberbia attempts to seduce Entendimiento, but is rejected,

> por saber yo que en pecando
> se convierte el hombre en bruto.†[4]

† This symbol indicates that an English translation is given in the Appendix, pp. 106–22.

3. Calderón, *Los encantos de la Culpa*, p. 408.

4. Ibid., p. 411.

The senses, we learn, have been converted into brutish beasts
by the blandishments of la Culpa's ladies-in-waiting; when
el Hombre finds out what has happened, he knows that he is
in trouble, and he appeals to Entendimiento for help:

> Hombre: Docto Entendimiento mío
> en gran peligro me veo;
> a mis deseos deseo
> rescatar con mi albedrío
> para vivir, pues que yo
> de aquí no puedo ausentarme,
> que no tengo de dejarme
> compañeros que me dió
> mi misma naturaleza.
> Y supuesto que perdidos
> todos mis cinco Sentidos
> están en esta aspereza
> de la Culpa, entrar intento
> a libertarlos, porque
> bien de la empresa saldré
> si voy con mi Entendimiento.†[5]

Entendimiento agrees to help him, but on three conditions: el
Hombre must confess his guilt, he must ask heaven's pardon,
and he must repent. He does these things, the doing of which
ushers in another character, la Penitencia, to the accompani-
ment of music and song:

> (Tocan chirimías y cantan)
> Músicos: Ya que el hombre confiesa su culpa
> y arrepentido me pide perdón,
> ¡oh, Penitencia!, pues eres el Iris,
> acude volando a darle favor.†[6]

La Penitencia appears, and, in a poetic exchange of great
beauty, gives el Hombre a vase of flowers, which represents
the seven virtues. El Hombre and el Entendimiento set out to re-
cover the senses, which they find living in a pig-heaven. La
Culpa, with the help of la Lascivia, tries to tempt el Hombre;
but realizing that this is impossible while el Entendimiento is
present, she contrives to send el Entendimiento away with the

5. Ibid.
6. Ibid.

reluctant senses. Then she offers el Hombre, now alone, all the delights of knowledge and sensuality:

> La Culpa: De las flores te leeré
> estos escritos cuadernos
> donde la Naturaleza[7]
> escribió raros misterios.
> A todas horas tendrás
> dulces músicas, oyendo
> suaves cantos de las aves,
> de los hombres dulces versos.
> Sabrosísimos manjares
> te servirán con aseo
> tal, que el olfato y el gusto
> se estén lisonjeando a un tiempo.
> La vista divertirás
> en esos jardines bellos,
> que son nuestros paraísos
> de varias delicias llenos . . .
> . . . Y sobre todo tendrás
> los regalos de mi pecho,
> las caricias de mis brazos,
> los halagos de mi afecto,
> las finezas de mi amor,
> la verdad de mi deseo,
> la atención de mi albedrío,
> de mi vida el rendimiento;
> y finalmente, delicias,
> gustos, regalos, contentos,
> placeres, dichas, favores,
> músicas, bailes, y juegos.†[8]

While listening to this, el Hombre lets fall the flowers of virtue given him by la Penitencia, and he succumbs. Entendimiento returns in dismay, and there follows an antiphonal song in which Entendimiento argues against pleasure while the musicians in the service of la Culpa reiterate the joys of sensuality. The competing refrains are "Acuérdate de la muerte" and "Acuérdate de la vida." El Hombre, who still has the power to

---

7. It need hardly be said that a "naturaleza" thus manipulated by la Culpa, is, as nature always is in Calderón's work, a fallen creation.

8. Calderón, *Los encantos de la Culpa*, pp. 415, 416.

choose, chooses again; with the aid of la Penitencia, he chooses to remember death. With his senses regained, he sails off, while la Culpa and her court fall victim to an earthquake and a flood, understanding full well, and even lauding, the divine power they have been unable to overcome.

Los encantos de la Culpa illustrates, vividly and insistently, several articles of faith: earthly joy is transient; sin is bestial; man can choose, with the aid of his reason, between this world and the next and thereby be saved. This message is stated outright in lessons and made concrete in dramatic events that give theatrical life to certain conditions of existence and encompass specific rituals, such as the eating of the bread of the Eucharist. The play's arrangement calls special attention to the possibility of free choice; el Hombre has not one, but two, chances to redeem himself through acts of will, and Calderón directs his dramatic effects toward making these occasions memorable. The choice offered to el Hombre is unambiguous; he may either listen to his Entendimiento or to his senses. Since the correct choice is a foregone conclusion, a matter of dogma, the play presents no really difficult conflict; nor does it contain any ideas, theological or experiential, that are in any sense original. What it does contain is much impressively ornate language and stage activity. One's response to this ornateness depends upon one's opinion of its suitability to the feelings expressed. It is certainly possible for a reader of a certain taste to consider the play too florid to purvey an ascetic message. Calderón is a worldly ascetic, if such a contradiction in terms is permissible; like other baroque artists, and like the Jesuits under whom he was educated, he is open to the charge of excessive ostentation. But this ostentation itself can convey an ascetic message. The world of *Los encantos de la Culpa* is not fulfilling, it is seductive, a garden for the flowers of evil. If sin is glamorous, salvation must be competitive; and in Calderón's theater it is. This is not subtle theology, but it is powerful emotional manipulation, based upon a credible view of the human appetite. Calderón's religious and dramatic premises are fully sanctioned by Loyola's *Spiritual Exercises*, about which Francis Fergusson has written:

> The *Spiritual Exercises* of Ignatius Loyola . . . reveal,
> through the techniques of make-believe, the potentialities of

human nature and the realities of the human situation, as Loyola understood them. When he explains to the devout how to make present to their feelings and imaginations as well as their reason, scenes from the life of Christ, he sketches a technique like that which the Moscow Art Theater used to train actors. His immediate purpose is similar: to reveal a scene significant on many levels, and a mode of action capable of evoking a mimetic response of the whole being.[9]

The force and beauty of Calderón's play derive from its imaginative and, in the manner of the *Spiritual Exercises*, sensual illustration and theatricalization of what was thought to be the reality of human nature. That this reality may seem partial does not detract from the intensity of the dramatic effect.

In *Los encantos de la Culpa,* Calderón divides, for the purpose of dramatic representation, something that is empirically indivisible: a human personality. By isolating and making concrete what are essentially inalienable and intangible qualities (the senses, the reason, the sense of guilt), Calderón can enact an internal conflict in such a way as to make it comprehensible and conceptually very clear. He has separated psychological, moral, and emotional conflicts into two competing actions, one enacting license, the other, control. The real battle is between el Entendimiento and la Culpa. El Entendimiento's victory might be more difficult to convey on a plane other than this allegorical one, where divine forces, by intervening decisively, provide the means of salvation.

As *Los encantos de la Culpa* celebrates the rational ordering of the human personality, so another *auto, El gran teatro del mundo,*[10] upholds not only personal self-control, but also the order of society. To this end, Calderón establishes a social hierarchy, the members of which are rewarded with a divine approval, bestowed in the form of salvation given in return for a lack of social presumption, or (to put it more positively) for a belief in the moral correctness of the ethical demands placed upon each member of a divinely ordained society in which each

9. Francis Fergusson, *The Idea of a Theater* (Princeton: Princeton University Press, 1949), p. 237.
10. Pedro Calderón de la Barca, *El gran teatro del mundo,* in *Obras completas,* 3:199.

individual serves his own interest best by being true to his own role and showing concern for his fellow men.

El gran teatro del mundo, like *Los encantos de la Culpa*, is an effective piece of manipulative theatrical didacticism that pleases in its mimetic representation of partial truth. It is typically Calderonian both in its radical inventiveness and in its conservative thematic preoccupations. Calderón's adeptness in handling a classical myth in *Los encantos de la Culpa* is here matched by a masterful elaboration of the conceit conveyed in the title: the world as theater. The idea that all the world is a stage carries implications of its own, which Calderón's treatment must limit and define. The title's idea can be understood to mean that human life is vain posturing. When the conceit appears in Shakespeare it carries this connotation; but Shakespeare represents this as merely one point of view, and not a very encompassing one. If one assumes that there is something about life that is not theatrical, some reality that is not illusion, some world about which man can know the truth, then one must concede that the world is *not* a stage. In *El gran teatro del mundo* the idea that the world *is* a stage is expressive of Calderón's vision; but this "world" is also real, since it has been created and is controlled by God. Human life does have meaning, but only in that it conforms to a divine plan. The stage world of *El gran teatro del mundo* is an exposition of that plan, and it is meant to be more real than the illusory world perceived by the senses.

The stage world of *El gran teatro del mundo* encompasses both the divine and the human. God is the *autor* of the play; he creates a character, el Mundo, with whom other characters interreact in a way like that in which human beings respond to their world. The relations between el Mundo and the characters are subject to divine intercession, which comes in the form of una Voz. The cast is typed not only according to abstract qualities of spirit (la Hermosura, la Discreción), but also according to specific social roles (el Rico, el Rey, el Labrador, el Pobre) that are given as fixed entities; the characters are judged finally not by the relative social position they have been given, but according to their fidelity to the standards of behavior set, by heavenly writ, for all time, for that position. Every character, no matter what his place, must remember that this life is but a preparation for the next and hence must not place his faith in its pleasures. It is within each character's power to be true to his part:

> Labrador: ... y pues Tú sabes, y es llano
> porque en Dios no hay ignorar,
> qué papel me puedes dar,
> si yo errare este papel,
> no me podré quejar de él:
> de mí me podré quejar.†[11]

God intervenes to insure that each character knows the choice he must make to insure his salvation:

> Autor: Para eso, común grey,
> tendré desde el pobre al rey,
> para enmendar al que errare,
> y enseñar al que ignorare,
> con el apunto, a mi Ley;
> ella a todos os dirá
> lo que habéis de hacer, y así
> nunca os quejaréis de mí.
> Albedrío tenéis ya,
> y pues prevenido está
> el teatro, vos y vos
> medid las distancias dos
> de la vida.†[12]

Some of the characters (who, like human souls in Church doctrine, have existed in potential before having been assigned specific roles in the theater of the world) complain of the parts they have been given. Especially moving is the complaint of el Pobre:

> ¿Porqué tengo de hacer yo
> el pobre en esta comedia?
> ¿Para mí ha de ser tragedia
> y para los otros no?
> ¿Cuándo este papel me dió
> tu mano, no me dió en él
> igual alma a la de aquel
> que hace el rey? ¿Igual sentido?

11. Ibid., p. 207.
12. Ibid., p. 209.

> ¿Igual ser? Pues, ¿por qué ha sido
> tan desigual mi papel?†[13]

This question, which reminds one of nothing so much as Segismundo's opening complaint in *La vida es sueño*, provokes the predictable response: death will equalize. El Pobre must suffer, indeed; but his misery will be rewarded with salvation, while el Rico, who has every reason to be thankful for the role he has been given, grows too fond of pleasure ("Comamos hoy, y bebamos,/ que mañana moriremos" †),[14] and for this he must burn in hell.

The social doctrine illustrated in this play conforms utterly to that of the Catholic Church of the Middle Ages. (The reader who desires a thorough analysis of the doctrines illustrated in this play should read *The Allegorical Drama of Calderón* by Alexander A. Parker, an exposition and defense of Calderón's *autos*.) All the issues presented in the play have obvious doctrinal solutions; and the manner of their presentation is nothing more, nor less, than a matter of aesthetics. (The questions answered in *El gran teatro del mundo* involve technical matters such as: "How many stanzas should be devoted to a poetic exposition of human history?") So it is not fruitful to ask, as Shelley did, whether this or any other of Calderón's *autos* is "true," because it is true to a Catholic Counter-Reformation vision of this world and of the next. The question to ask about *El gran teatro del mundo* is: Is it beautiful? To put the question in this way might seem, to a believer, to be condescendingly entering into a still vital area of belief. But it can be argued that the play's greatest virtues are other than religious or didactic.

Calderón has justified his allegorical art as the means by which theology can be related to human experience:

> sé que quiere Dios
> que, para rastrear lo inmenso
> de su Amor, Poder y Ciencia,
> nos valgamos de los medios
> que, a humano modo aplicados,
> nos puedan servir de ejemplo.
> Y pues lo caduco no

13. Ibid., p. 208.
14. Ibid., p. 217.

puede comprender lo eterno,
y es necesario que, para
venir en conocimiento
suyo, haya un medio visible
que en el corto caudal nuestro
del concepto imaginado
pase a práctico concepto:
Hagamos representable
a los teatros del tiempo.†[15]

As this passage states, Calderón works down from a "concepto imaginado"—based upon what he thinks is the truth of God's "Amor, Poder y Ciencia"—to a "práctico concepto," a play. The sequence is revealing. One might wonder what religious value there might be in an art based upon what seems to be the author's satisfied knowledge of God's workings and wishes. In *El gran teatro del mundo*, Calderón's self-assurance is such that he puts God on stage as if He were a known and fixed thing to be associated with other known things perceived by the faculty of reason. Such a process is inimical to modern religious thought and modern aesthetics, although it is true, as Parker demonstrates, to the Scholastic tradition that Calderón maintains as if he were unconcerned with the religious and critical theories that had begun even before his time to refute the most fundamental principles of his *autos*. But if one wishes to find more to admire in Calderón than his ingenuity as an illustrator, and there is more, he must perceive a tension between what Calderón does and what he does not do, between what he says and what he leaves out.

Calderón's aesthetic erases real human society in order to deal with, and celebrate, a "concepto imaginado," a traditional idea of social order. This conception cannot hope to embody temporal human reality. Whether it can embody an eternal reality is, of course, questionable. To Calderón, it can. To agree with him is to enable oneself to see in the *autos* "the play of the Lord," a play that is a plausible total picture of a timeless universe. To disagree is to see the play of Calderón, a play in which a single human sensibility creates a God, a universe, the

15. Pedro Calderón de la Barca, *Sueños hay que verdad son*, in *Obras completas*, 3:1215.

choirs of heaven, and the furniture of the earth in order to respond to his own condition as a man living in society and in
time.

El gran teatro del mundo is a joyous and playful work. Even
el Rico's final speech, delivered as he is sent to eternal torment,
has a celebrative tone:

> ¡Ay de mí! Que envuelto en fuego
> caigo arrastrando mi sombra
> donde ya que no me vea
> yo a mí mismo, duras rocas
> sepulturán mis entrañas
> en tenebrosas alcobas.†[16]

El Rico knows the layout of his eternal dwelling, and he is not
at a loss for words to describe it; his rhetoric is surely more
referential than expressive in its treatment of real human suffering, although it is appropriate to a joyful exposition of God's
workings. Calderón works easily in the world of "conceptos
imaginados." His autos exclude a direct perception of the world
in which he himself lives and of which he writes in his comedias.
Temporality is the very substance of Lope's comedia, and
Calderón must have understood this. His playing with fixed
fancies does not imply an ignorance of the world, but it implies
a rejection of it; this brings artistic freedom of a sort, but it
conveys, above all, an unwillingness or an inability to deal successfully with the problems of living in time. His comedias are
documents of that inability, and they exhibit nothing like the
game-playing, chesslike ease of the autos. In his comedias he
attempts to reconcile the timeless with the temporal, and in his
failure there is much of interest and much to be learned.

16. Calderón, El gran teatro del mundo, p. 222.

La vida es sueño

Calderón gives *La vida es sueño*[1] a universal setting in a distant land, but he keeps the shape and meaning of the action close to home. The play's main plot enacts, in characteristically Calderonian fashion, a challenge to the social order and the subsequent containment of that challenge; the parallel and complementary subplot restores, through marriage, the honor of a wronged woman. *La vida es sueño*, with its almost limitless philosophical suggestiveness, is much richer than a descriptive chart of its ideology would show; but, for all its complexity, it works up only a few ideas. Some of the most vividly drawn actions are suppressed in the end, though the reasons for this, at least in terms of the explicit argument, are good ones. Here, as everywhere in Calderón's theater, stage action is less a direct imitation of human action than it is an illustration of a preconceived idea of its meaning. And here, as much as anywhere in Calderón's works, or in those of any playwright, the conceptions are particularly impressive, especially those that enact man's attraction to woman and his desire for liberty. One almost wishes that a genius more liberal than Calderón's had possessed the powers of poetic conceptualization so evident here, for it cannot help but disappoint (though not surprise) that his unbending fidelity to the inseparable values of honor and order should prohibit the union of the play's two main characters and thus suppress the author's intuition of the heart so that a reason of state can be upheld. And it is disappointing that a play that will always have an appeal because of its impressive rhetoric of liberation should so utterly reject libertarian principles in the end.

Such disappointments are inevitable, since Calderón's intensity is bought at the cost of liberality of vision. His conceptualizations may shine brilliantly, but they are fixed and

1. Pedro Calderón de la Barca, *La vida es sueño*, in *Obras completas*, 5th ed., vol. 1, ed. A. Valbuena Briones (Madrid: Aguilar, 1966), p. 501.

atemporal, unsuited to development or growth. Freedom and order, earthly joy and divine reward, revolt and repression, dreaming and reality—all are absolutes to Calderón. They can be kept in an uneasy equilibrium within a personality, a polity, a stage action, an entire play, or a single speech; but they cannot be reconciled. One must choose, and Calderón's characters choose in favor of control. What else could be expected from the characters in a play written by an author whose syntax shows a difficult but total conquest of the most far-flung rhetorical opposites?

In *La vida es sueño* the value of the correct choice is enhanced by the perverse attractiveness of what must be rejected. Calderón's readers will always have sympathy for what is renounced, as long as liberty and love and life are valued; but to Calderón, order is a higher value than any of these. To Calderón the human appetite is dangerous. In *La vida es sueño*, the portents, actions, and images associated with Segismundo's natural inclination are emblems of upheaval. The play opens with a consummately antiromantic image of nature: a runaway horse, which, for all its violence, is kept under a tenuous but viable control by Calderón's extravagant but never illogical rhetoric, just as, throughout the play, eruptions are kept in place and balanced with their opposites to make a whole that is coherent and ordered, though curiously strained. Segismundo's emotions are violent in the extreme:

> En llegando a esta pasión
> un volcán, un Etna hecho,
> quisiera sacar del pecho
> pedazos del corazón.†[2]

As the play progresses, his feelings become, if possible, more intense, but they remain essentially the same:

> Ah, cielos,
> qué bien hacéis en quitarme
> la libertad; porque fuera
> contra vosotros gigante
> que para quebrar al sol

---

† This symbol indicates that an English translation is given in the Appendix, pp. 106–22.
2. Ibid., p. 502.

> esos vidrios y cristales,
> sobre cimientos de piedra
> pusiera montes de jaspe.†[3]

As the passage above implies, and as Segismundo states explicitly elsewhere ("sé que soy/ un compuesto de hombre y fiera" †),[4] the dangerousness of his natural impulses is patent, evident even to him. When he is released, destructive actions result: attempted rape, defenestration, and revolt.

It is also true, however, that Segismundo has been unjustly imprisoned, which is to say, in the terms of Calderón's conceptual argument, that violence can be fostered by, or at least is paradoxically coterminous with, the agencies of state control and the limitations of human nature (for which man cannot be held responsible). Segismundo's imprisonment in the tower is both the cause and the effect of his violence. The blame for his condition is not his, yet he must suffer the consequences. Consequently, his expostulation to the heavens is a justified complaint against the limitations dealt him by the powers responsible for the human condition (or rather, the human condition as it might appear to mortals who have yet to discover and seize an opportunity to elect their own salvation):

> Apurar, Cielos, pretendo,
> ya que me tratáis así
> qué delito cometí
> contra vosotros naciendo;†[5]

Segismundo's imprisonment has resulted from an astrological forecast that Calderón represents as unjust because in its inherent determinism there is a denial of free will. Even Basilio, the stars' agent in Calderón's Poland, knows that will can overcome limitation:

> cuánto yerro ha sido
> dar crédito fácilmente
> a los sucesos previstos;
> pues aunque su inclinación
> le dicte sus precipicios,
> quizá no le vencerán,

3. Ibid., p. 504.
4. Ibid., p. 516.
5. Ibid., p. 502.

porque el hado más esquivo,
la inclinación más violenta,
el planeta mas impío,
sólo el albedrío inclinan,
no fuerzan al albedrío.†[6]

The theological questions involved in Segismundo's predicament, and Calderón's enactment of them, are most certainly of
interest; but it must be recognized that Calderón has answered
the play's questions before the fact. La vida es sueño is arranged in such a way as to call attention to a paradoxical
predicament, to make it as vivid as possible, and then to solve
it. Through most of the play (exactly how much does not really
matter), the activities, human and poetic, are aligned with one
or the other of two static, mutually irreconcilable, partially
justifiable ideas of human action: action as revolt or action as
containment. After a while (it does not matter when) Calderón
steps in and halts the conflict by giving his character an opportunity to make a choice.

There is in La vida es sueño what might be taken as the
beginning of a dialectic involving freedom and restraint. It
could be argued that Segismundo's imprisonment is a circum-
stance that contains a contradiction, in that it fosters the forces
that will undo it. From the conflict between repression and rebellion, it would seem, a new stasis, or synthesis, might be
produced. It is true that Segismundo, after his conversion, does
incorporate into his character the restraint that had previously
enslaved him. Can this be called a synthesis? In fact, it is an
excision and a recombination. What had been, until Segismundo's conversion, a constraint imposed from without, becomes internalized. Segismundo chooses to restore, unaltered,
the forms of authority that had been essential to the political
order he had previously threatened. A series of stage events
that restores the status quo ante cannot be called dialectical,
nor can it be said to embody a developing action. It embodies
a very carefully enclosed action—an illustration of a conflict
that does not change in time.

There is a chain of apparent causes and effects in La vida es
sueño. Segismundo's experience must teach him to make the
correct choice when the time comes, and Calderón must pre-

6. Ibid., p. 508.

sent that experience in such a way as to make the choice appear to be reasonable. Segismundo bases his choice upon having had the experience of realizing that life is a dream; he chooses to renounce pleasure and to start behaving as a responsible and austere Christian prince. Before one addresses the rightness of Segismundo's chosen course, one should take note of how, and how well, Calderón demonstrates that life is like a dream.

It could be maintained that Calderón merely chooses to illustrate an arbitrary preconception about life and that his vision is not much different from that of many Counter-Reformation ascetics whose ideas are now of historical interest. Some of Calderón's most perceptive readers have rejected entirely the ideas his plays advance. Such was the case with the nineteenth-century English essayist G. H. Lewes. Lewes quotes part of Segismundo's central soliloquy:

¿Qué es la vida? Un frenesí.
¿Qué es la vida? Una ilusión.
Una sombra, una ficción.
Y el mayor bien es pequeño;
que toda la vida es sueño,
y los sueños sueños son.†[7]

Then he remarks (with an aggressive concern that Calderón's theater deserves, but has rarely elicited since):

This is a fine burst of poetry, but the philosophy is neither new nor true; and if it *were* true, if this life *were* all illusion, all a sick and troubled dream, would not the task of the philosopher still be the same—to discover our relations to the universe and to each other?[8]

Lewes is right in asserting that Calderón's "philosophy" is borrowed, but Calderón is not to be judged as a philosopher; he is a playwright. If he does not *discover* "our relations to the universe and to each other," he at least offers a credible conception of them. And yet it still may be argued that his conception is too limited to be of much interest. This is Lewes's real objection, and it has been echoed by Américo Castro. Castro has had very little to say about Calderón, but what he

7. Ibid., p. 522.
8. George Henry Lewes, *Spanish Drama: Lope de Vega and Calderón*, p. 176.

has said is, as is often the case with Castro, pithy and illumi-
nating. In *De la edad conflictiva* he writes: "Calderón poetizó
su idea de no ser el hombre como la naturaleza, de no poseer la
soltura de los animales, de hallarse, en definitiva, en manos de
Dios, no ligado a un cosmos."[9] In a footnote, he adds: "Prescin-
damos del carácter ingenuo de esta idea de Calderón acerca
de la naturaleza y de la libertad."[10] Castro, like Lewes, holds
a low opinion of Calderón's "philosophy," that is, of his
thought. Castro's motive in citing Calderón's "ingenuous" idea
about nature and liberty seems to be to hold it up as an example, as an indication of the paralysis that could be said to
have overcome Spanish intellectual life in the seventeenth century. Yet Castro's professed motive for having written what
he has about the literature and social history of Calderón's
time is not that he wishes to diagnose lingering social diseases
(although he does do that), but rather that he hopes to show
how the creation of certain works of literature had been made
possible by historical conditions and socially induced states
of mind. Calderón's *idea* (which cannot even be said to be his
own) is certainly ingenuous (or, at least, limited); but, as
Castro implies in his act of *prescindimiento,* Calderón's theater
is somehow more important than the explicit ideas it promotes.
One might not choose to imagine one's life in the symbolic
terms Calderón offers. One might not care at all whether life
is or is not like a dream, or whether man has the freedom of
the animals, or whether sufficient grace may be provided at the
right time to enable man to use his will to elect salvation; yet
one still might be interested in the means by which Calderón,
as Castro says, *poetiza* (makes poetry of) these ideas. Still more,
one might be interested in the meanings conveyed in *La vida
es sueño* in addition to the ones that are explicit and doctrinaire.
Within the play, Calderón must establish a situation in which
Segismundo may realize, on the basis of some experience, that
human life is illusory. This realization is orchestrated effec-

9. "Calderón made poetry of his idea that man is not like the rest of
nature, that he does not possess the freedom of the animals, that he finds
himself, definitively, in God's hands, not bound to a cosmos." Américo
Castro, *De la edad conflictiva,* p. 223.

10. "Let's overlook for the moment the ingenuousness of this idea of
Calderón's concerning nature and liberty." Ibid.

tively by Calderón through the presentation of a convincingly distorted picture of life in a dramatic language that undercuts the reality of what is being signified.

Rosaura's first speech places the events in a "confuso laberinto" from which the characters may escape only after Calderón has enforced his resolution to their problems. Until then, almost nothing is clear to any of them; they move in a half light ("la medrosa luz que aún tiene el día" †)[11] or in the full glaring spotlight of the court, with their necks craned upward toward the heavens to receive the answers to their perplexing dilemmas. Clotaldo, at the end of the first act, might be speaking for any of the characters when he says:

> Descubra el Cielo camino;
> aunque no sé si podrá,
> cuando, en tan confuso abismo,
> es todo el cielo presagio,
> y todo el mundo un prodigio.†[12]

Segismundo moves with all the quickness of a dream from imprisonment to liberty, back to imprisonment, and finally once again to freedom. It is the rapidity of these changes that leads him to doubt the reality of his experience. His mental states, and the actions that issue from them, are volatile; they are beyond his conscious control until he is enabled to see their unreality and to reject, once and for all, his untrustworthy desires. Perhaps the most typically Calderonian poetic analogies in *La vida es sueño* are Segismundo's repeated visions of unstable realms: the "república inquieta/ de las aves" and the "inquieta república de estrellas."

The verbal action of Calderón's poetry dissolves the reality of the world as it is perceived through the senses and substitutes a world of fantastic verbal entities. Clotaldo does not threaten Rosaura and Clarín with an ordinary pistol, but with an

> áspid
> de metal [que] escupirá
> el veneno penetrante

11. Calderón, *La vida es sueño*, p. 501.
12. Ibid., p. 510.

de dos balas, cuyo fuego
será escándalo del aire.†[13]

When Segismundo contrasts his enslavement to a bird's liberty,
he speaks of no ordinary bird:

Nace el ave, y con las galas
que le dan belleza suma,
apenas es flor de pluma,
o ramillete con alas†[14]

In these passages, and throughout the play, Calderón associ-
ates fixed quantities through qualities they hold in common,
giving a new perspective from which each one may be seen.
The effect derives from the distance between the two things
compared; each one loses some of its substantiality because
each depends upon its association with another for its poetic
reality. The vision of life conveyed by this language can hardly
be called ingenuous; on the contrary, it is effective and intense.
Perhaps the *idea representable* that underlies the play is naive,
but the enactment is not. It is no accident that readers first
becoming acquainted with *La vida es sueño* almost invariably
become enthralled with Calderón's great conception and enactment of life as a dream, with his dramatization of a state of
anxiety and anguish; only after some logical reflection do they
see the play's weaknesses, which show themselves upon consideration of Calderón's proposed cure for the state of anxiety.

The purpose of the dreamlike life Calderón creates is, one
can assume, to prepare Segismundo for his decisive choice of
the next world over this; outside the play, it is to convince
the spectator that *his* world is essentially dreamlike too. Segismundo's dream and Calderón's play are instruments of *desen-
gaño*. If the play were an *auto sacramental*, Segismundo, upon
awaking from his dream, would be visited by a character, such
as la Penitencia, who would offer him the means of salvation.
In fact, there *is* an *auto* with this same title in which something
like this occurs. However, this play is not an *auto*, and it presents no purely allegorical characters; nor does it allow for
divine participation. The intervention is Calderón's; he arranges Segismundo's conversion, and he uses the character of

13. Ibid., p. 504.
14. Ibid., p. 502.

Rosaura as the agent of that conversion. At a decisive point, when the destinies of Segismundo and Rosaura converge, Segismundo chooses to "obrar bien" in two distinct ways, which Calderón connects by having them occur at the same time. There is no compellingly logical reason why the two should go together. Segismundo's decision to renounce his attraction to Rosaura in order to cleave unto the eternal ("¿Quién por una gloria humana/ pierde una divina gloria?"†)[15] need not necessarily lead him to become her champion nor to begin adopting the restraints that had been working upon him from the outside. It does not follow, at least from what the reader is given to know of Segismundo's involvement with Rosaura, that he should all at once become the guardian of the established order. He does so because Calderón has decided to associate these two activities. If life is a dream, it might indeed be better to eschew it temptations, but why then must this accompany a conversion to belief in the reality and necessity of earthly institutions? The question was first asked by Italian Hispanicist Arturo Farinelli:

> Il dramma, che si disse sgomentevolmente serio e di vertiginosa profonditá, offre gli strappi piú vivi ad ogni seria e profondo riflessione. Corra il pensiero da una parte, e corra dall'altra l'azione drammatica, il poeta non se ne preoccupa. Ditegli che nel mondo del sogno dell'illusione deve porsi anche l'onore, ed egli si ribellerá al vostro e al suo proprio giudizio. Nulla di chiaro riesce a veder l'uomo nell'universale fantasmagoria, anzi non vede punto; gli si confonde ogni cosa nell' indistinto del sogno; e Calderón obbliga tuttavia a chiaramente distinguere il raggiar dell' onore nella vita morale degl'individui e della societá. E, in conclusione, trasmuta il dramma del sogno della vita nel dramma dell'onore restaurato . . . Onore, lealtá, fedele sommesione al sovrano, gentilezza, cortesia, convenienza sociale, ordine, compatezza di vindoli nella famiglia e nello stato, misura, vedete quanto si salva dal complesso delle larve vane che costituiscono il mondo e la vita terrena nell'oscillar di tutto, ammirate tanta stabilitá di principi. Se il mondo scompare, rimani la legge.[16]

15. Ibid., p. 530.
16. "The drama, which is said to be terribly serious and of a vertiginous depth, offers debilitating shocks to all serious and profound reflec-

Farinelli's objection seems to hold up, if one regards Calderón's
lack of fidelity to the concept that "life is dream" as a major
flaw in the play. But, in spite of the play's title, it does not
demonstrate that life is a dream, merely that life is *like* a dream.
Calderón is no skeptic. He makes sure that both Segismundo
and the audience understand that Segismundo's experiences in
the palace have *not* been dreams, but rather experiences that
in their evanescence have been like dreams. The lesson to be
learned is that life is as untrustworthy as a dream. Thus it is
not difficult to accept Segismundo's conversion into an upholder of firm, eternal principles. Calderón reifies the eternal
in the appointments of civilization. The order that Segismundo
embraces is a necessary protection against the chaos that
Segismundo has had a metaphorical dramatic realization of in
his dreamlike experience and that has its verbal correlative in
Calderón's style. As Calderón controls language, so he controls
action; both are inherently chaotic, and he subjects both to
rigid conceptual constraints. These are the reality; they exist
before and after all difficulties of perception; all else may be
doubted, but they may not.

Edward M. Wilson, in an article partly devoted to defending
Calderón's play against Farinelli's objections, has rightly
pointed out that Farinelli's expectations must inevitably produce disappointment when held against Calderón's apparent
intentions. Wilson (in an attempt to find value in the play
other than the value Farinelli deals with) has written:

> Can the play as a whole mean anything to those who do not
> share the religious outlook of the author? I think it can. . . .

---

tion. The thought runs in one direction, the dramatic action in another;
the poet doesn't care. If you were to tell him that in the world of dream
and illusion honor should remain, the idea would repel your and even his
own judgment. In the universal phantasmagoria man can discern nothing
with clarity, he can't see a thing, everything is confused in the indistinct-
ness of the dream, yet Calderón nonetheless obliges him to distinguish
clearly the rays of honor in the moral life of the individual and of society.
And in conclusion, he transforms the drama of the dream of life into the
drama of honor restored . . . Honor, loyalty, faithful submission to the
sovereign, gentility, courtesy, social convention, order, sympathy for the
bonds of the family and the state, moderation—look at how much is
saved from the complex of vain phantoms that make up earthly life in
its total mutability, admire so much stability of principle. If the world
disappears, the law remains." Arturo Farinelli, *La vita è un sogno*, 2:185.

> We are not yet able to feel that there is no conflict between our
> impulses and our reason; we have still to come to terms with
> the world in which we live. Calderón was conscious of these
> problems, he stated them, and he gave us a solution to them.
> His statement is of the greatest importance to us, whatever
> we think of the solution.[17]

To this I would add that the attitude itself is embodied in the
solution. Even if one does not accept the solution, he should
look carefully at Calderón's statement of the problem. Wilson
might recognize the truth of human impulses and human reason in Calderón's play, but if I were to take a stand on this
matter I would say that Calderón's truth is not true; it is a
distortion, made with an end in mind and as a response to a
felt need. One does not read Calderón to find out about the
world, or the reason, or human appetites; one reads Calderón
to experience his tortured and unsuccessful attempt to make
what is unreasonable seem reasonable and to put up some sort
of defense against an ever-present and barely controllable will
to disorder.

In a freely willed act, Segismundo represses his own unruly
nature and simultaneously ends the social upheaval. The rewards are great. He regains his own liberty (within limits that
are now self-imposed); restores Rosaura's honor and the well-
being of the polity; and he upholds all the values catalogued by
Farinelli (*onore, lealtá, gentilezza, cortesia,* etc.) as being essential to Calderón's vision of how the world should be. There is a
cost. To Segismundo the cost is, in part, Rosaura. He does not
marry the heroine, and he cannot, because *raison d'État* requires
that she marry Astolfo, the man who dishonored her, and that
Segismundo marry Estrella, the princess. There are plays (one
thinks first of Racine's *Bérénice*) in which such an outcome
might be considered the stuff of tragedy. In *La vida es sueño,*
Segismundo's loss is not tragic, it is in some sense a triumph.
His attraction to Rosaura has been, on the whole, bestial, and
when not bestial, illusory. To him, she is either the object of
rape or a "breve cielo," stunning but unearthly; except, that is,
when she is preceived as a defender of her honor. Her struggle
to restore her honor gives her a dignity and importance not

17. Edward M. Wilson, "On 'La vida es sueño,'" in *Critical Essays on
the Theatre of Calderón,* ed. Bruce W. Wardropper, p. 89.

inherent in her condition as a woman. There is no equal, or even nearly equal, claim given to honor and love; in fact there is no fully developed love in *La vida es sueño*. But there is a continual and overtly stated sexual fascination that links Segismundo and Rosaura, although Calderón does not elaborate on it.

Segismundo's choice is too easy; there is not enough lost; he is too self-satisfied at the play's close. It is one thing for a man to lose the whole world to gain his soul; it is quite another thing for him to seem unaware of the loss. Life may be like a dream, but if woman is real (and Segismundo says so: "Sólo a una mujer amaba. . . / Que fue verdad, creo yo,/ en que todo se acabó,/ y esto no se acaba"†),[18] then the playwright has some obligation to pursue the implications of her reality. He seems to imply that there is something between Segismundo and Rosaura that is more real and enduring than the spectacle around them, but he can take that implication no further. He seems willing simply to let the possibility of their love live for a while on stage, only to have it die when the time comes to put all the pieces together at the end. It is true that Rosaura's effect upon Segismundo may be interpreted as an uplifting one; she shows him the path of honor and restraint. But this interpretation—although it holds to the general argument of the play, in which love does not matter—does not explain away the sense of dissatisfaction one feels at Calderón's sudden abandonment of the erotic action he has begun. His characters seem to have no trouble renouncing their claims to each other's lives; but in forcing their renunciations, Calderón has introduced a problem into his theatrical world that he is apparently unable to handle: the problem of love.

La vida es sueño can be read as an attempt to circumvent logic through a defensive affirmation of the principles of order. These principles show themselves to be inadequate. Whether Calderón sees them as inadequate is perhaps doubtful; they are the only answers he offers. The play is less effective in demonstrating the logic of repression than it is in displaying an intuition of chaos, and its overall effect is to make one wonder whether this upheaval, as conceived by Calderón, can be controlled at all.

18. Calderón, *La vida es sueño*, p. 522.

Had Calderón shown himself capable of mastering, rather than simply intimating, the actions of Eros and the workings of social forces, he might have been able to lead *La vida es sueño* to a less arbitrary and more encompassing resolution. But, to Calderón, love is linked with aggression and change is inseparable from violence; to reject one he must reject them all. His strengths are other than those of Lope de Vega. Where Lope transcends conflicts between order and spontaneous affection, Calderón intensifies them. In his language he continuously attempts to contain the strongest emotions by using the most rigid intellectual constructions, with the result that one senses the violence more strongly. The polarities are resolved, but at the expense of great distortion, and the solutions reached are unstable. Segismundo's victory over himself, the victories of the state over anarchy, of duty over love, and of eternal values over earthly ones, are difficult and ultimately debilitating. Nevertheless, they prevail, and in their prevailing they are not tragic.

Segismundo resolves to live out his life without love, as a sober servant of the morality of restraint:

> ¿Qué os admira? ¿Qué os espanta,
> si fue mi maestro un sueño,
> y estoy temiendo, en mis ansias,
> que he de despertar y hallarme
> otra vez en mi cerrada
> prisión? Y cuando no sea,
> el soñarlo sólo basta;
> pues así llegué a saber
> que toda la dicha humana,
> en fin, pasa como sueño,
> y quiero hoy approvecharla
> el tiempo que me durare† [19]

One might wonder whether Segismundo's satisfaction in his newly won equilibrium is more convincing than the fact of his reduced humanity and Calderón's statement of how threatening that humanity has been. The reader may decide for himself whether Calderón's atemporal and reduced world is a paradise; Calderón does not draw that conclusion. Segismundo's

19. Ibid., p. 533.

new kingdom is safe, perhaps, until a new threat appears; but its security depends upon a subdual of those impulses that may lead mankind, until it is therapeutically *desengañado*, to seek fulfillment, however partial, in earthly life. This subdual may be a necessary condition of survival, at least in the play's terms; still one wishes that Calderón had shown a more complex understanding of the taste for the life, however illusory, that he forces his characters to give up. *El príncipe constante* is in this respect a more satisfying, and on the whole a better, play.

El príncipe constante

There is perhaps no play that better demonstrates Calderón's sureness in setting forth already-defined ideas than *El príncipe constante*;[1] yet this play offers much more than a merely coherent and predictable philosophy. In the poetry of *El príncipe constante*, Calderón possesses imaginatively, and concretely, a complex and ambivalent vision that the play's ready-defined, "illustrated" concepts do not succeed in limiting.

Most of the play's commentators have reduced it to its ideological framework. The English critics have shown, not incorrectly, that the prince Don Fernando exemplifies the virtue of fortitude as defined by St. Thomas Aquinas;[2] the adoptive Americans Reichenberger and Wardropper have demonstrated, with some accuracy, that Fernando's martyrdom and apotheosis make the play not a tragedy, but rather something like an *auto sacramental* in which an exemplary man elects to suffer on earth in order to defend and exalt the kingdom of God.[3] It may be superfluous to reiterate the ways in which these judgments can be affirmed, but since in their partial truth they are essential to an understanding of the control and the complexity of Calderón's total (and, it may be said, tragic) vision in this play, it is perhaps not out of place to state them here.

El príncipe constante carries the message that human life is not enough, that one must look to the eternal to find a reality more constant than the fleeting glories of this world, which are destroyed by time:

1. Pedro Calderón de la Barca, *El príncipe constante*, in *Obras completas*, 5th ed., vol. 1, ed. A. Valbuena Briones (Madrid: Aguilar, 1966), p. 245.

2. See especially Albert E. Sloman, *The Sources of Calderón's "El príncipe constante."*

3. See Arnold G. Reichenberger, "Calderón's *El príncipe constante*, a tragedy?," pp. 688–70; and Bruce W. Wardropper, "Christian and Moor in Calderón's *El príncipe constante*," *Modern Language Review* 53 (1958): 512–20.

Al peso de los años
lo eminente se rinde;
que a lo fácil del tiempo
no hay conquista difícil.†[4]

As in *La vida es sueño* and in the *autos*, Calderón here arranges
the action to enable his character to choose among alternatives,
which are conceived as dualities: world versus eternity, sensuality versus denial, life versus death, inconstancy versus constancy. In *El príncipe constante* these are embodied in actions
that do not precisely coincide with the characters' religious and
cultural affiliations. Some Christians, including even Fernando's brother, the prince Don Enrique, waver in their belief in
God's constant purpose (when Enrique falls to the ground as
he first sets foot in Africa, he takes it as a bad omen and must
be reassured by Fernando);[5] while a Moor, Muley, shows signs
of fidelity that are real and genuine, if compromised by his
inability to abandon worldly concerns. Fernando alone gives
up the world. His motive in martyring himself is superficially
a worldly one; he is unwilling to be responsible for the loss of a
part of the Christian empire, Ceuta. This tells of a higher motivation, a constancy and fidelity to eternal values that brooks
no compromise with any of life's temptations. Calderón presents Fernando's martyrdom in such terms as to show its
moral superiority to the variously self-interested actions of the
play's other characters. There are many terms of exchange in
the play (*rescate, precio, valor*), all of which, in unequal equations, show that Fernando, whatever his worldly condition,
is worth more than any of the play's other characters. Fernando's moral worth grows as his earthly misery increases; he
is worth the most when he is dead; at the end, his corpse out-
values Fénix's still untarnished beauty. Through renunciation
he achieves glory. Ergo, it can be argued that the play is not
tragic. As Reichenberger says:

† This symbol indicates that an English translation is given in the
the Appendix, pp. 106–22
4. Calderón, *El príncipe constante*, p. 249
5. Fernando: Pierde, Enrique, a esas cosas el recelo,
                    porque al caer agora, antes ha sido
                    que ya, como a señor, la misma tierra
                    los brazos en albricias te ha pedido. † Ibid., p. 254.

> *El príncipe constante* lacks the one essential quality for
> tragedy, catastrophe at the end. Fernando is a flawless
> character who lives unflinchingly by a code of hierarchically
> arranged values, both secular and religious. His death, chosen
> by himself in the exercise of his *libre albedrío*, is the logical
> conclusion of his Christian constancy. His re-appearance as
> a spirit after death brings on the triumph of right. Fernando
> is a martyr and a saint, but not a tragic hero.[6]

To take this view is to limit the play unnecessarily. To call
Fernando a "flawless character" may be relevant to an attempt
to hold Calderón to a neo-Aristotelian model, but why must
that attempt be made? Fernando may not be flawed by hubris
in the neo-Aristotelian sense (hubris is in fact not an Aristo-
telian idea, but rather a Renaissance idea based on a misunder-
standing of Aristotle); he is not flawless, however, insofar as
he is human. If one is to rely upon neo-Aristotelian precepts
(Reichenberger mentions Aristotle's medical metaphor of "ca-
tharsis"),[7] he might easily miss the point of Fernando's humanity, which makes his torment fully as important as "the
triumph of the right." There is a "catastrophe" in *El príncipe
constante*; the play depicts a painful action, great suffering,
and the death of the hero. In responding to this one should
decide whether the "tragic" must be limited to a more or less
self-centered, self-pitying response to the difficulties of life
(Reichenberger speaks of the "blind cruelty of uncontrollable
forces")[8] or whether it may be found, as Calderón finds it (and
in this he is closer to Aristotle than the neo-Aristotelians are)
in a view of life that makes certain values seem more important
than life itself. That Fernando, as a witness to the transcendent,
should be redeemed in another life does not remove the fact
that he has suffered, inevitably it may be said, for the limitations of his humanity and the insufficiency of the world. There
is no reason to make an incomprehensible universe an abso-
lute requisite for tragedy. In *La vida es sueño*, where a character
also renounces something for the sake of a transcendental order,
there is no tragedy because neither Segismundo nor Calderón

6. Reichenberger, "Calderón's *El príncipe constante*," p. 670.
7. Ibid.
8. Ibid.

seems aware of the value of what is renounced and because life
and the state are kept intact. In *El príncipe constante* the suffering and the loss are felt. While *La vida es sueño* leaves one
feeling somewhat disappointed with its ethic of survival
through partial renunciation, *El príncipe constante*, because it
is uncompromising, has an exalting effect; it leaves one with a
sense of enhanced understanding, if not of vitality.

One might object (as one might object in regard to the *autos
sacramentales*) that the beauty of *El príncipe constante* is static,
achieved through the pursuance of an illustrative course. Calderón, sure of the transience of human life, frees himself to
recreate its decadent luster; at the same time, equally sure of
the clement action of a divine presence, he illustrates, in exemplary tableaux, the path of transcendence. One can almost
respond to *El príncipe constante* by dismissing it as another,
though less florid than most, exercise in ornamental didacticism; one might almost conclude that here, as in the *autos*, Calderón has attempted, through the exercise of sheer aesthetic
power, to enact an impossible ideal and make it convince by its
celebrative vividness alone. This judgment must surely follow
an acceptance of the thesis held by Reichenberger et al. that
the play is a sort of hagiographic spectacle. However, such a
judgment is insufficient to explain the doomed love between
Fernando and Fénix, the *divina imagen*, that is Calderón's love
affair with the world. Here the choice between the world and
the spirit is not made simple, and its dramatic working out is
not hampered by ideological fixity; it seems *discovered* in a way
that only the playwright's attempt to understand himself could
make possible.

Calderón invests the character of Fénix, and the world
around her, with a kind of erotic fascination that attracts Fernando, until she and the world fail him and he must leave them.
The play's subtlety involves the fascination, its moral the failure. Although Fénix is beauty incarnate, she is also incomplete.
She can't enjoy her own beauty or understand her melancholy;
she is uncomprehendingly fatalistic about the course of her
life. In her first speech she asks for a mirror; what she sees in
it doesn't help her:

> ¿De qué sirve la hermosura
> cuando lo fuese la mía

> si me falta la alegría,
> si me falta la ventura?†[9]

In her self-centeredness she cannot connect her emotions with those of others (this shallowness is brought out perfectly in the captive's question: "Música cuyo instrumento/son los hierros y cadenas/ que nos aprisionan, puede/ haberla alegrado?"†);[10] she remains a passive melancholiac:

> Solo sé que sé sentir;
> lo que sé sentir no sé;
> que ilusión del alma fue.†[11]

When a divining hag predicts that Fénix's beauty, which is her essence, will be the price of a man's life, her response is self-pitying credulity and fatalism. This is in sharp contrast to Fernando's confident purpose, which leads him to dismiss omens as *miedos vanos* (idle fears).[12] The fate that overcomes her, as predicted by the hag, is perhaps equivalent to a "tragic" destiny as it might be conceived by one who sees it in the suffering imposed on humanity by a hostile, inscrutable universe. That is how she regards it. To Calderón, however, this is not a tragic view, but a self-indulgent and ignorant one. Through the actions of Fernando, Calderón attempts to demonstrate that the world is not ruled by chance, but according to divine values that can be understood and acted upon.

Fernando's generous and constant faith enables him to accept his own suffering, to feel that of others as well, and to read the message of nature and the world (as in the sonnet upon the *maravillas*) with an understanding of what must be lost. Fernando knows how to die ("morir como buenos,/ con ánimos constantes"†);[13] and his death has meaning, painful as it is. If there is tragedy anywhere in Calderón, it is here. It may even be said, to those whose precepts require that the tragic hero confront the "blind forces of an uncontrollable destiny," that those forces, in Calderón's vision, have made the world and human consciousness so insufficient, even unendurable, that they can

9. Calderón, *El príncipe constante*, pp. 250–51.
10. Ibid., p. 250.
11. Ibid.
12. Ibid., p. 255.
13. Ibid., p. 258.

be escaped only through death, and that suffering and dying, finally, are desired:

> Fernando: ¡Oh, si pudiera
> mover a alguno a piedad
> mi voz, para que siquiera
> un instante más viviera
> padeciendo!†[14]

In *El príncipe constante*'s probable source, *La fortuna adversa*,[15] which was perhaps written by Lope de Vega, there is an amorous episode between a Moorish queen and a Christian prince, but it is crudely presented; the queen is licentious, the prince, virtuous to the point of self-righteousness. In Calderón the issues and the actions are more complex. Fénix is no crude temptress to be rejected easily, she is a real temptation in her beauty and in her implied role in the working out of Fernando's destiny. Fénix and Fernando are linked explicitly in the soothsayer's prediction, in the contrast between her self-centeredness and his magnanimity, and in the parallel development of her physical beauty with its moral helplessness and his physical degradation with its spiritual force. More significant than any of these, however, is the muted love that they begin to show for one another (which, if Calderón's didacticism had won out over his emotional complexity, might never have appeared).

Fernando has known what it is to love ("sé qué es amor");[16] his response to Muley's complaint ("Fénix es mi pensamiento")[17] is to state that compared to the pains of love his own are slight ("si Fénix su pena es/ no he de competirla yo"†).[18] This might be simply an expression of kindness and reticence, but it might also indicate a real relief at being able to cast off the world and its erotic temptations. Yet his relief is premature, for her beauty does attract him. The course of Fernando's martyrdom is almost wholly plotted when he meets Fénix in the garden; he is figuratively a dead man when he first meets her (his "gerundive" character, as of one who is to die, is implied

14. Ibid., pp. 250–51.
15. Reprinted in Albert E. Sloman, *The Sources of Calderón's "El príncipe constante,"* which includes a discussion of the authorship of *La fortuna adversa*.
16. Calderón, *El príncipe constante*, p. 257.
17. Ibid., p. 261.
18. Ibid.

from the beginning of the play), and yet there is more to this scene than a self-confident farewell to an uncomprehending image of worldly temptation.

The garden scene opens with Fénix's wonderings about the import of the hag's prediction:

> Fénix: ¡Precio de un muerito! ¿Quién vió
> tal pena? No hay gusto, no,
> a una infelice mujer.
> ¿Que al fin de un muerto he de ser?
> ¿Quién será este muerto?†[19]

She is more anxious about her future status as a "precio" than about the "muerto" for whom she shall be exchanged, except insofar as death and mortality are frightening and vile to her. The ellipsis in her speech ("de un muerto he de ser?") seems purposeful on Calderón's part; her failure to begin the clause with the expected "precio" implies a closer kind of belonging than mere exchange, an implication strengthened by Fernando's terse response as he enters with a bouquet:

> Fernando: Yo.[20]

This "Yo," whatever it might tell us of Fernando's spiritual superiority in his foreknowledge and acceptance of death, is also the direct statement of his loving presence.[21] Fernando and Fénix have not even been introduced in the play, yet he announces himself as if his bond to her were stronger than any considerations of social nicety. The exchange that follows is intense:

> Fénix: ¡Ay Cielos! ¿Qué es lo que veo?
> Fernando: ¿Qué te admira?
> Fénix: De una suerte
> me admira oírte y verte.
> Fernando: No lo jures, bien lo creo.
> Yo, pues, Fénix, que deseo
> servirte humilde, traía
> flores, de la suerte mía

19. Ibid., p. 266.
20. Ibid.
21. This interpretation of the garden scene derives from that of Leo Spitzer, which can be found in his article "Die Figur der Fénix in Calderón's *Standhaften Prinzen*."

jeroglíficos, señora,
pues nacieron con la aurora,
y murieron con el día.
Fénix: A la maravilla dió
ese nombre al descubrilla.
Fernando: ¿Qué flor, di, no es maravilla
cuando te la sirvo yo?
Fénix: Es verdad. Di, ¿iquién causó
esta novedad?
Fernando: Mi suerte.
Fénix: ¿Tan rigurosa es?
Fernando: Tan fuerte.
Fénix: Pena das.
Fernando: Pues no te asombre.
Fénix: ¿Por qué?
Fernando: Porque nace el hombre
sujeto a fortuna y muerte.
Fénix: ¿No eres Fernando?
Fernando: Sí soy.†²²

This dialogue, in spite of its formal structure and its allegorized
subject matter, gives a sense of intimate interaction. The *maravilla*, a hieroglyph of Fernando's fate, may belong, as is almost
always the case with Calderón, more to the realm of symbols
and concepts than to nature; still it is a real flower. Fernando,
like the *maravilla*, is soon to die; but his act of bestowing a
flower upon a florid princess as the token of a "dead" man's
love is an act of some poignancy. The pain Fénix feels on receiving Fernando's gift, along with his implied, understated
gift of awareness (the awareness of one who is, unlike her, a
slave, but like her in subjection to fortune and death), holds at
this point the promise of becoming a kind of release from her
isolation, through their shared understanding of the meaning
of suffering and also, and equally important, through their loving contact. Fernando's concern for her feelings is at the same
time an implied request that they achieve a state of identification with each other; it may be read not just as a lesson to her
in how to deal with mortality but also as the declaration of love
from a man who knows he is about to die. It is Calderón's last
offer of love to the world, and it is believable.

22. Calderón, *El príncipe constante*, p. 266.

One might wonder why Calderón, even in such an understated way, here introduces hope that there will be a resolution in love rather than in death. Curtailed loves occur in other plays by Calderón: in *La vida es sueño* the hero's fate is linked with that of a woman in a common action that involves love and that, in its necessary conclusion, separates the lovers forever for the sake of a social necessity; in *El mágico prodigioso*, Cipriano and Justina consummate their love not on this earth, but rather in the pure realm of martyrdom and apotheosis. In each of these plays, love is something other than love; it is a mysterious catalyst that incites the spiritual faculties and leads to a renunciation of sexuality and to a dedication to a higher purpose. In *El príncipe constante*, Fernando, a man already pledged to a martyr's death, offers a hopeless love to Fénix, to beauty and the world, inviting her to partake of his superior vision and to join him in another life. She fails him, and her failure is embedded in the very heart of the play.

There is an apparent doctrinal clarity to the sonnets (the play's lyrical core) delivered upon Fernando's bestowal of the flowers:

> Fernando: Estas, que fueron pompa y alegría,
> despertando al albor de la mañana,
> a la tarde serán lástima vana,
> durmiendo en brazos de la noche fría.
> Este matiz, que al cielo desafía,
> iris listado de oro, nieve y grana,
> será escarmiento de la vida humana:
> ¡tanto se emprende en término de un día!
> A florecer las rosas madrugaron,
> y para envejecerse florecieron:
> cuna y sepulcro en un botón hallaron.
> Tales los hombres sus fortunas vieron,
> en un día nacieron y expiraron;
> que pasados los siglos, horas fueron.†[23]

Fénix reacts with fear ("Horror y miedo me has dado"†)[24] and rejection; she shreds the flowers. In judging her response one must take into account Fernando's words and the misery of his condition. He does not offer an easy path to transcendence,

23. Ibid.
24. Ibid., p. 267.

but rather a grim reminder of his own mortality. Without the implied but unstated reward of eternal life, his vision of the meaning of life is fearful; and her reply draws a moral from mutability other than the one implied by Fernando:

> Fénix: Esos rasgos de luz, esas centellas
> que cobran con amagos superiores
> alimentos del sol en resplandores,
> aquello viven que se duelen dellas.
> Flores nocturnas son, aunque tan bellas,
> efímeras padecen sus ardores;
> pues si un día es un siglo de las flores,
> una noche es la edad de las estrellas.
> De esa, pues, primavera fugitiva
> ya nuestro mal, ya nuestro bien se infiere:
> registro es nuestro, o muera el sol o viva.
> ¿Qué duración habrá que el hombre espere,
> o qué mudanza habrá, que no reciba
> de astro, que cada noche nace y muere?†[25]

The two sonnets, which have such a similar verbal substance, exemplify the two opposing world views that the play enacts. Fernando is to turn his awareness of the brevity of earthly things into a solid reliance upon the eternal. He renounces the world, but he never doubts the reality of God's purpose. Fénix fears the mysteries of a universe that is to her unknowable, her melancholy grows fror her inability to perceive the vague designs of kismet, which are written, she thinks, in the stars. But even in Calderón's explicit presentation there are complications; since, from any point of view on this side of the grave, the heaven Fernando hopes for is distant, and the suffering needed to attain it is intense. And even to one pledged, as Fernando is, to suffer for a sure and superior purpose, Calderón makes it difficult to renounce beauty's attraction. The equation of Fernando's spiritual beauty with Fénix's earthly perfection, as stated for the last time in the play by Fernando's brother, is still ambiguous, curiously unresolved, and, for Calderón, nondidactic:

> D. Alfonso: Rey de Fez, porque no pienses
> que muerto Fernando vale

25. Ibid.

> menos que aquesta hermosura,
> por él, cuando muerto yace,
> te la trueco. Envía, pues,
> la nieve por los cristales;
> el enero, por los mayos;
> las rosas por los diamantes,
> y, al fin, un muerto infelice,
> por una divina imagen.†[26]

Fernando's final resurrected appearance, when he is shown clothed in church vestments and waving a flaming torch at the head of the Christian armies, is certainly a lapse into obviousness and a point for debate by those who would deny that the play is tragic. But Calderón's literal-minded religion is something that must be dealt with and accepted as a functioning part of his work. Fernando's spiritual values, which are so complex throughout the course of the play, are in the end made concrete in what seems like a caricatured Santiago de Compostela—a picture that robs the play of much of its mystery. The apotheosis is so broad, in fact, that one might wonder whether it is to be believed, or whether there is not such a great effort at forcing belief that a certain insecurity shows through. Readers of Calderón have been and will continue to be bothered by his easy theology; he seems to have all the answers, and the answers have material equivalents. But it helps to remember that he works within established forms, reworking and altering established ideas. There is less to be learned from the ending itself than from Calderón's manner of arriving at the ending; what happens is not as interesting as how it happens and how much the audience has to accept in addition to what they had expected.

Since it is safe to say that scarcely any modern reader would find Fernando's resurrection a plausible occurrence, it is worth examining what remains of the play if one rejects its outcome. Albert Camus, in the introduction to his translation of *La devoción de la cruz*, states, with an insight that might as easily have been inspired by a reading of *El príncipe constante*, that to dissever man from destiny is to deliver him to chance.[27]

26. Ibid., p. 278.
27. "Mais c'est plus de trois siècles avant Bernanos que Calderón prononça, et illustra de façon provocante, dans la *Dévotion*, le 'tout est

The destiny Calderón provides for Fernando is so literal, so essential, that to remove it is indeed to deliver him to chance. Chance is precisely what Fénix is all about. Her character exemplifies the perfect human world without divine providence, fickle and mutable; and if to that world one were to add a gratuitous and unrewarded suffering of the kind Fernando undergoes (which in Calderón's play, however, is rewarded), one is left with a vision of a world destroyed by time and human inadequacy. Calderón's world is either redeemed by his literal theology or it is lost utterly, and his poetic vision points to the possibility of loss. El príncipe constante's forced ending and its repressed eroticism underline the tenuousness of Calderón's answers to the anguish his play sets forth. Martyrdom is not reconciliation; its joys are not human joys; its rewards are not as readily discernible to mortals as is the reality of the suffering it entails.

In the serious plays of Calderón men suffer and die, and they are not happy. There is an answer to their unhappiness, but it is a drastic one, to be reached only through willful rejection of the world and adherence to the path of transcendence that God, through Calderón's intervention, provides. Calderón's characters find that the most difficult of their human impulses to manage is their sexuality; this is a problem both to Segismundo and to Fernando, and of course the problem is Calderón's. In La vida es sueño, Calderón drops the issue of Eros at a crucial point in the play; in El príncipe constante he keeps it alive but fails to resolve it, until finally it looms so large that its lack of resolution turns what seems to be a simple ideological vehicle into something more ambiguous. Whatever is lasting and valuable in El príncipe constante lies in that ambiguity. But the play is still not completely satisfactory. It succeeds, like all Calderón's better plays, in honestly setting forth an action in which a dearly held idea engenders (as a consequence of its being invoked and upheld in the face of the world and the flesh) a contradiction that cannot finally be resolved in the terms of

---

grâce' qui tente de répondre dans la conscience moderne au 'rien n'est justé des incroyants." ("But it is more than three centuries before Bernanos that Calderón pronounced, and illustrated in a provocative way, in the Devotion, that 'grace is everything' which attempts in the modern consciousness to respond to the 'nothing is just' of the unbelievers.") Albert Camus, La dévotion á la croix, in Théatre espagnol (Paris, 1953).

the initial exposition. The play does not create a new vocabulary with which the choices it discovers may be completely understood. Instead it invokes answers that are meant to be timeless responses to timeless dilemmas but that are in fact bound to a state of culture at a specific time in history. It may be idle to ask more of a playwright, but the example of Lope de Vega serves as an easy contrast to Calderón, for Lope's theater will live at all times, not just in those times, such as our own, in which Calderón's bleak vision of the world coincides with an existential despair. *El príncipe constante* does not reach the level of Lope's greatest works, principally because Calderón does not have Lope's intuitive understanding of the heat and pulse of human action and love. Love enters through the back door in Calderón's plays, and it never really finds a home other than in the doomed action of a dead man's charity or in the puzzled imagination of a dreaming prince, who upon awakening to a higher reality will cease to imagine or to love. And a world without love cannot forever be a Christian world; Calderón finally fails the religion he seeks to exalt. Lope's *El caballero de Olmedo*, like *El príncipe constante*, reenacts in human form the passion and death of Christ.[28] In Lope's play, the hero's death at the hands of humanity finds meaning in its analogy to the death of Christ, which, like Alonso's, is a loving consummation. The principal difference between Lope's play and Calderón's is that in the former Eros and caritas can each find a place on earth, while in the latter (perhaps through a failure not in the lover but in the world itself) they cannot. Lope suggests the passion of Christ in Alonso's passionate love; the rhythm of spiritual transcendence is carried in the love itself, not, as in Calderón, in the mastering or abandoning of the love. Lope's Alonso does not begin to comprehend the transcendental meaning of his own death; what is not human for him retains its mystery. Calderón takes the mystery out of the divine and injects it instead into the confusion of a contradictory world, in which love can be intuited but cannot be realized, in which the eternal can be known but cannot be made sufficient. Lope's reticence in giving answers to metaphysical questions may be seen, perhaps, as an evasion of the issues Calderón

28. For the development of this interpretation, see Willard King's introduction to her edition and translation of *El caballero de Olmedo, The Knight of Olmedo* (Lincoln: University of Nebraska Press, 1972).

faces squarely; but in fact it is not, for to one for whom life has meaning, death is not an end in itself, it is a mystery beyond our understanding that can be justified only in its correspondence to the passions of which it is the culmination and which it cuts short. Calderón, in trying to explain life from beyond the grave, has presumed too much. Even with Calderón's literal salvation, the world of men as it appears in his plays is a beautiful but fallen creation, a void. Without that salvation, the void extends to encompass the universe.

La dama duende

La dama duende[1] is probably the best known of Calderón's cape-and-sword comedies. It is also one of the most highly regarded of all Golden Age plays of its kind. The play deserves its renown; as a piece of theater it is playable and amusing, it shows its author's mastery in creating and controlling the complexities and ironies of incident that the genre requires, and its language is clear. These qualities are what one expects from a work by Calderón. He is a great technician; his plays, when they resemble earlier *comedia* types, have a quality of summation. In their technical competence they seem to perfect the forms they adopt in a way that confirms Calderón's position as the consummator of a great tradition. Such a designation is more misleading than it is accurate, however; *La dama duende* differs in its essential spirit from the plays, especially those of Lope de Vega, that make up the tradition to which it seems, superficially, to conform. Calderón's play is neither as funny nor as lyrically inventive as many of Lope's comedies; it lacks Lope's embarrassment of riches, but it offers clarity in exchange. Along with this clarity it offers a degree of penetration in its handling of the honor issues implicit in the form, issues that Lope (because he is not interested in such matters, or because they gain importance only if regarded by one who distrusts the power of love) ignores or circumvents. Calderón takes honor seriously as a necessary agency of control. The honor intrigue in *La dama duende* is not amusing, nor may its consequences be avoided easily in the playful pursuit of love. In *La dama duende* the enforcers of the honor principle are both prurient and puritanical; they exhibit extremes that are either absent or made ludicrous in Lope's characters, although they may be implicit in the values that Lope's plays accept through evasion. Calderón's reworkings of the *comedia*, with

1. Pedro Calderón de la Barca, *La dama duende*, ed. H. Koch (Halle: Saamlung romanischer Uebungtexte, 1952).

their changes of emphasis and their acuteness in confronting the consequences of the *comedia*'s conventional actions, are social and moral criticisms of the kind that Lope avoids or, perhaps, transcends through a celebration of sexual love. The flashes of lust followed by flashes of guilt and repression that Calderón's characters experience lead to situations that require the imposition of a strong social sanction to handle the guilt and to keep the lust under control.

When compared with Lope's *capa y espada* comedies, *La dama duende* shows its limitations. The play lacks Lope's spontaneity, its twists of plot are mechanical, and its metaphors proclaim the clichélike character of many of the most common *comedia* turns of language. Comedies of this type should exist on lighthearted love poetry if nothing else. Calderón offers something else: a moral seriousness that seems out of place in such a play and yet is at the same time arresting. There is a dissonance in *La dama duende* between vehicle and message that is so typically Calderonian that it can be regarded as an anomaly only within the context of the *comedia* (in which context any of Calderón's plays is an anomaly). An audience expecting to find in *La dama duende* what it finds in Lope's comedies, might, if its attention is only superficial, find the expected, presented more dryly, less lovingly, or less lyrically; but closer attention reveals certain axiological contradictions. In offering such a revelation, Calderón is true to his own form and no one else's.

In *La dama duende*, love competes with honor as a young widow, Doña Ángela, struggles to free herself from the protectiveness of her two brothers. Such a competition is hardly unusual in a cape-and-sword comedy, but here love and honor are more ambiguously presented than is the case in the plays of other *comedia* playwrights. This is not a sly celebration of the victory of Eros over social compulsion;[2] it is rather a demonstration of the inadequacy and insufficiency of each and of their fundamental irreconcilability on any terms other than those imposed by a sacrament.

As love and honor conflict, each exacerbates the other; and in the confusion provoked by their interaction it is difficult to

2. See Lope's *La viuda valenciana*, in which honor and reputation are treated as no more than complications in a sympathetically conceived sexual intrigue.

see how one is separable from the other. Each can be justified on its own terms, but neither is fully justified. Doña Ángela's brothers, because they are concerned about their honor, keep her a prisoner in her own house. This is excessive, certainly, and even hypocritical; but, more significant, it is not effective. It fosters the rebelliousness they seek to control. Her situation is like that of Segismundo in the tower. She *is* dangerous. Not for nothing is she called *la dama duende* and likened, throughout the play, to a demon. But the implication is that she is more demonic because she has been held in check, her resources restricted to those of trickery. Her brothers, too, for all their concern for honor, have explosive and barely controlled carnal appetites. As guardians of order and morality they are far from pure. Don Luis, in particular, is a contradictory character whose zealousness in protecting his sister's good name is matched by his own prurience and a scarcely concealed incestuous desire for her. In *La dama duende*, as in all of Calderón's comedies, characters "fall in love" as if they are contracting a disease that reaches its critical stage within minutes. The ideology of honor is not sufficient to control the disease—in fact, it worsens it by distorting the erotic impulse, making it conform to a narrow rule of right and wrong behavior, and feeding a sense of guilt by forcing dissimulation.

Doña Ángela's justifiable but dangerous recourse to trickery leads, through many intricate deceptions, some of them amusing, to a situation that is not really funny. Don Manuel, the play's hero and straight man, finds himself, through no fault of his own, caught in a compromising position with the woman, having offended both brothers' sense of honor, having violated the obligations of friendship with one of the brothers, and having been placed in a situation where he must defend the honor of a woman he does not know but whom he feels obliged to protect. His loyalties are split, and it seems that the outcome will be bloody:

Don Manuel: Hidras parecen las desdichas mías
al renacer de sus cenizas frías.
¿Que haré en tan ciego abismo,
humano laberinto de mí mismo?
Hermana es de don Luis, cuando creía
que era dama. Si tanto (¡ay Dios!) sentía

ofenderle en el gusto,
¿que será en el honor? ¡Tormento injusto!
Su hermana es: si pretendo
librarla, y con mi sangre la defiendo,
remitiendo a mi acero su disculpa,
es ya mayor mi culpa,
pues es decir que he sido
traidor, y que a su casa he ofendido,
pues en ella me halla.
Pues querer disculparme con culpalla,
es decir que ella tiene
la culpa, y a mi honor no le conviene.
Pues ¿qué es lo que pretendo?
¿Si es hacerme traidor si la defiendo:
si la dejo, villano;
si la guardo, mal huésped: inhumano,
si a su hermano la entrego?
Soy mal amigo si a guardarla llego;
ingrato, si la libro, a un noble trato;
si no la libro, a un noble amor ingrato.
Pues de cualquier manera,
mal puesto he de quedar, matando muera.
No receles, senora; (A Doña Ángela)
noble soy, y conmigo estás agora.†[3]

Faced with a choice between a social obligation and an obligation of the heart (which, it should be noted, is also more
social than emotional), Don Manuel is about to choose to follow the latter, whatever the cost. But, as is always the case in
such situations in Calderón's plays, the cost is sure to be high.
To die for love may be a noble thing to a hero in a tragedy by
Lope de Vega (Calderón's heroes never do it), but here such an
act is out of place. Its suggestion, in fact, is self-negating; it
serves to show how impossible it is to act when love and liberation are the motives: the consequence is death, *morir matando*.
A way out short of death must be found, and it is: marriage.
The marriage is suggested by Don Luis, Doña Ángela's repres-
sor; and it is significant that this should be so, for the marriage

† This symbol indicates that an English translation is given in the
Appendix, pp. 106–22.
3. Calderón, *La dama duende*, p. 116.

is congruent with the set of honor values that has been invoked by Doña Ángela's brothers throughout the play to keep Eros in check. It is apparent that, for Calderón, freedom, love, and death are to be feared.

In his treatment of honor in *La dama duende*, Calderón reveals his paradoxical attitude toward social restraint: it is both disagreeable and finally necessary. The play might be taken as an indirect "criticism" of his society's honor code (many critics have taken his "honor plays," which differ little, in their treatment of honor, from *La dama duende*, as such a criticism). Honor as enforced by Doña Ángela's brothers operates with oppressive cruelty. Yet her anarchic defiance carries the action to a point at which nothing less than a strong social restraint can contain it, and here Calderón tips the balance. He gives restraint a higher authority; he "divinizes" the human institution of honor (just as he makes the state sacrosanct in *La vida es sueño* and legitimizes revenge in *El médico de su honra* by having the king give his approval).

Although authority insures stability, it also, curiously, fails to eradicate the reader's sense of the injustice practiced throughout the play by the agents of control. One remembers that state power has kept Segismundo in prison and that Don Luis, whose authority is upheld at the end of *La dama duende*, has himself chased his sister in incestuous passion through the streets of Madrid when he thought he had her locked up safely at home. In Calderón's plays, social control is something greater than the individuals who practice it. The image of those individuals, or of society itself, that remains in the reader's mind after Calderón has justified them is still an image of arbitrary actors in a world in which, in Camus's words, nothing is just. After Calderón, with a certain lack of believability, announces the "happy" ending, there remain in mind images of a confused world peopled with hot-blooded hypocrites and dangerous femmes fatales. Is this Calderón's criticism of Spanish society? What can be affirmed is that although *La dama duende* criticizes society through its very existence as a play built upon the theatrical conventions of social comedy, to its inherent format it brings a vision of the world that is too anxious and ascetic to allow one to take comfort in the nuances of emotional and social behavior. Such nuances and little acts of forgiveness, so common to Lope's plays, escape Calderón.

He shows a society without cohesion and in need of an imposed order. This is a criticism of society, but it is also a self-criticism; for Calderón's loveless world is of his own making, even though he is peculiarly capable of suggesting the need for what his art cannot or dare not affirm: human trust and love.

El médico de su honra

El médico de su honra[1] belongs to that group of Calderón's plays, the honor plays, that for the past two centuries has provoked from most of his readers an extraordinary fascination and disgust. Calderón did not invent this genre; he wrote only three real honor plays, and he wrote them at a time at which the form was already mature, if not overripe. But because his honor plays, although they lack anything like the spontaneous turns of language that grace even Lope's slightest efforts, are the best, the most dramatically coherent and exciting plays of their kind, and because their kind has come to be regarded as embodying an uncritical and therefore repellent exposition of an inhuman social practice, Calderón's reputation has taken much of the blame for the entire collective enterprise, social and literary. His honor plays have been called barbarous, tasteless, and cold. They have been taken to exemplify the narrowness, bigotry, and mechanical repressiveness existing in some sections of Spanish society before, during, and since his time. Typical, but not unique, are the damning parodies of Calderonian husbands in the works of such writers as Clarín[2] (in *La regenta*) and Valle-Inclán[3] (in *Los cuernos de Don Friolera*). Calderón's honor plays have been scorned by such disparate literary personalities as Menéndez Pelayo,[4] Unamuno, and Américo Castro.[5] Some recent English scholars have sought

1. Pedro Calderón de la Barca, *El médico de su honra*, in *Obras completas*, 5th ed., vol. 1, ed. A. Valbuena Briones (Madrid: Aguilar, 1966), p. 313.
2. La Regenta's husband, it is safe to say, does not comprehend Calderón well enough to see the ambiguities that certain modern critics have found in the honor plays.
3. Like Clarín's, Valle-Inclán's irony is best read as a criticism of his contemporaries' vulgarity and sexual hypocrisy, sometimes supported by the "classics."
4. See Marcelino Menéndez y Pelayo, *Calderón y su teatro*.
5. Américo Castro, *De la edad conflictiva*, p. 223.

to defend the honor plays with the premise that Calderón himself condemns the practice with which his detractors identify him. Alexander A. Parker, the founder of the so-called British school of Calderonians, has advocated a theory of "collective responsibility,"[6] which maintains that Calderón holds each member of society, each character in his honor plays, responsible for the play's action and outcome. Parker postulates, correctly, that social causes lend fatality to the honor plays, but he is unconvincing in his arguments about Calderón's intent. It is ultimately from within the honor values that Calderón finds his solutions to the problems of living in society. Honor must be maintained to keep order; although this may be unjust, it must be done. Justice must be found in heaven; the best that can be done on earth is to relate means to ends in order to ensure the provisional rewards of stability.

Analogies can be drawn between the Spanish honor values and other repressive ideologies. Honor is an abstraction, and devotion to an abstraction can distort the impulses and separate action from emotion. Honor is maintained through purgation; an attempt to "purify" a person, a state, or a family entails a projection of some detested attribute upon another and the elimination of the "other." Honor demands a concern for appearances. When it is threatened, it does not matter what the truth is; it only matters what others think. This leads to an effort to protect the appearance and to disregard the truth. The honor ideology and its consequences have been seen by social historians as essential elements of sixteenth- and seventeenth-century Spanish society: a devotion to abstract ideals; an attempt to purge the racially impure by means of the Inquisition (the avoidance of which, because of the threat of false accusation, required deception and concern for appearances); a need for cleverness and dissimulation just to ensure survival. Calderón expresses, in the anxiety of the characters caught within his honor plots, a pain that might have been felt, for slightly different reasons, by any member of his society, or by anyone who has lived in a repressive society. Is Calderón the enemy of such societies?

A modern awareness of the social conflicts of the Spanish Golden Age has brought attention to those writers who worked

6. Alexander A. Parker, "Towards a Definition of Calderonian Tragedy."

in the shadow of the Inquisition to create private works of affirmation or negation—the mystics, Rojas, the anonymous author of *Lazarillo de Tormes,* Fray Luis de León—and has magnified the achievement of Cervantes: his affirmation of freedom in the midst of necessity. Neither Calderón nor any other writer of *comedias* has benefited from this interest. The apparent attitude of the *comedia* writers is one of willing purveyance: "This is what you want; here it is." Writers of *comedias* can be considered critical only on the basis of what they force the audience to accept along with the expected affirmation of the generally held ideals, including the ideal of honor. Lope mitigates the honor ideal by skirting it with an amoral elemental erotic vision that can link antagonists through their common pursuit of Eros. His plays are not case studies of honor; they are plays about sexual love that usually involve an honor situation. Calderón's plays, also, deal with more than just honor; they deal essentially with sexuality, license, and control; but because control often coincides with honor and because control is everything to Calderón, he seems to be more seriously concerned with upholding honor than Lope ever is. But honor itself is an ambiguous value to Calderón; it is affirmed only as a last resort.

As a writer of *comedias,* Calderón has had to conform to audience expectations. Honor plays contain complete "casos de honra" that end in the elimination of the adulterous, or seemingly adulterous, wife. There are no exceptions. The characters are driven by necessity; they cannot *choose* to act (as the characters in Calderón's other plays can, no matter how foreordained their choices may seem), they *must* act to guard their honor. The need to maintain honor is a fatal need, one that requires an act of concealment and suppression once it even appears that honor may be lost. The fatality of the honor situation is the essential feature of these plays; it charges every action with an ironic meaning in that every action relates to the play's inevitable denouement, without which the characters and their actions make no sense at all. The husband, after some complaining, adopts the honor values and works according to their dictates to eliminate, in secrecy, the source of his anxiety: his wife. Since she is a cherished part of him, her elimination is his sacrifice. Once the purge has been completed, the king, as the source of moral authority, gives his approval and attempts to heal the situation by reintegrating the husband into a society made more whole and more stable through the husband's self-sacrificing act.

Calderón shows the loss that his characters must suffer as they bend their actions to adhere to an abstraction. In the honor plays, the husband loses his peace of mind, his wife, and his ability—if he may be presumed ever to have had it—to conceive of the world as anything other than a bloody theater of deception. If the character's loss is outvalued by the stability that is gained, there are always ambiguities for those who want to see them. In the honor plays the ambiguities are pronounced, the loss heavy, the reward hollow. Honor is finally an earthly ideal; it may serve to uphold a transcendental order, but it can do so only imperfectly.

Are not these plays, then, by virtue of their emphasis upon the unhappy outcome and the glaring contradictions of the honor-preserving action, in some sense indictments of the values they enact? Maybe. But a play about cannibals, even one that underlines the ghastliness of the practice, although it may foster the inference that cannibalism is itself horrible, might, if written by a cannibal, also emphasize the problems of protein shortage and overpopulation that make the practice necessary. It might be difficult for an outsider to perceive the tragedy of the situation, and he might project his own disgust into his conjectures about the intent of the cannibal-playwright. Calderón's view of the honor tragedy is an insider's view; he never departs from the honor values. If he were to depart to an extent that might permit him to treat sexuality as a force as creative as it is destructive, or freedom as anything other than a moral deviation, he might rightly be said to have a critical outsider's vision, and he might have been able to affirm something more than the authoritarian sanctions with which he ends his plays. But authoritarianism is always Calderón's resort; his plays do not break out of the literary and axiological limits within which they have been conceived, although they do stretch those limits and play upon the already known with an obsessive flair. Faith, honor, and country, the once-vital elements of the Spanish imperial vision, have not the strength in Calderón's plays to affirm themselves without leaving behind, on earth, a trail of blood and death.

* * * * *

The central question in *El médico de su honra* is: How can nature be controlled and its effects ameliorated? Nature's violence accompanies the actions of the prince Don Enrique (the lover of Mencía, dishonorer of Gutierre, and usurper of his brother's throne) and the reactions he provokes from the other characters: fear, excitement, love, jealousy, and despair. From the time, in act 1, when Enrique's upsetting presence is announced as he falls from his horse, through the king's final attempt at the play's close to enforce social and royal authority by absolving Gutierre and marrying him to another, it is the emotional assertion of the prince that brings forth the other characters' responses. These responses are the central actions of the play, and they are varyingly effective in the ways in which they handle the passions that the prince's acts embody and provoke.

Mencía's response to Enrique is one of fear, attraction, and confusion. Enrique's accident draws from her, as the play begins, a burst of dense, intense, and fatally passionate poetry:

> Doña Mencía: Desde la torre los vi,
> y aunque quién son no podré
> distinguir, Jacinta, sé
> que una gran desdicha allí
> ha sucedido. Venía
> un bizarro caballero
> en un bruto tan ligero,
> que en el viento parecía
> un pájaro, que volaba;
> y es razón que lo presumas,
> porque un penacho de plumas
> matices al aire daba.
> El campo y el sol en ellas
> compitieron resplandores;
> que el campo le dio sus flores
> y el sol le dio sus estrellas;
> porque cambiaban de modo,
> y de modo relucían,
> que en todo al sol parecían,
> y a la primavera en todo.

Corrió, pues, y tropezó
el caballo, de manera
que lo que ave entonces era,
cuando en la tierra cayó
fue rosa, y así en rigor
imitó su lucimiento
en sol, cielo, tierra y viento
ave, bruto, estrella y flor.†[7]

The sun and the spring here are abstract, formal elements
to be worked up in a verbal construct; they are less real but no
less passionate for their denial of what living experience says
they are and for their use here to play upon the relations that
words, concepts, and metrical patterns may have to each other
within a verbal world. The force of Mencía's outburst is both
intensified and harnessed by Calderón's artistic dominance.
The dramatic consequences of her passion will also be controlled and made lurid, as the power of her blood is transformed
from that of a living woman to the intense but congealed red-
ness of the stains upon her husband's hands.

Enrique's reappearance in her life, which rekindles an old
love forsaken for the sake of a marriage and introduces an irrational erotic force into the play, means death for Mencía;
and she knows it. (Calderón scarcely attempts to foster the
pretense that his characters themselves do not know what will
befall them as actors in a rigorously predetermined play; rather
he suggests the opposite by playing upon their own sense of
fatality, investing them with a horrified foreknowledge of what
is to come.) Mencía is the first to link her love to her death,
and the topic is taken up by Enrique as soon as he regains
consciousness:

Enrique: ¡Ay, don Arias, la caída
no fue acaso, sino agüero
de mi muerte! Y con razón,
pues fue divino decreto
que viniese a morir yo,
con tan justo sentimiento,
donde tú estabas casada,

† This symbol indicates that an English translation is given in the
Appendix, pp. 106–22.
7. Calderón, El médico de su honra, p. 318.

> porque nos diesen a un tiempo
> pésames y parabienes
> de tu boda y mi entierro†[8]

But the prince will not die. As a prince he cannot be the object of the husband's vengeance; and he is already figuratively beyond the control of his brother, the king. More important, the prince is the incarnation of nature herself (when Mencía asks in act 2 why the beasts do not protect her from him, he responds: "Porque de enojarme huyen" [Because fearing my wrath they flee from me]).

Mencía's response to Enrique is ambivalent and unconsciously incriminating. She asks him to return so that she may explain herself. His return leads to her husband's discovery of her actions and to his suspicion. She mistakenly feeds her husband's jealousy by pretending with too much protestation to have been alarmed by the presence of an intruder and by betraying an exaggerated fear of her husband's vengeance before he has had occasion to contemplate it. Her final mistake is to write to Enrique begging him to stay in Seville so that his flight will not be construed as involving her. Her husband surprises her in the act of writing and draws the inference she most fears. She pays for her confusion with her life. If not precisely "innocent" of all involvement with the prince (she is drawn to him), she is a victim, not just of society's code of honor, as some critics would have it, but of an emotional force that she cannot successfully withstand. Her intention to purify her virtue by testing it against a strong adversary is stated in act 1:

> Mencía: . . . solamente me huelgo
> de tener hoy que sentir,
> por tener en mis deseos
> que vencer; pues no hay virtud
> sin experiencia†[9]

This may be taken seriously as an honest expression of her motivation, although it does indicate a fatal ignorance of the power of nature and of the need for a stronger defense than that provided by good intentions.

8. Ibid., p. 320.
9. Ibid., p. 319.

That defense might be royal power, but unfortunately for all concerned, the king, Don Pedro, also lacks the ability to control his brother. The king's weakness and his estrangement from the other characters may be inferred from his abandonment of his brother at the play's outset, his defensive and ineffectual imprisonment of Gutierre and Arias after they have drawn swords in his presence, and his lack of success in persuading Enrique to stay away from Mencía once he learns from Gutierre that Enrique is suspect. With regard to this last matter, which is the play's central problem, the king means well; he tells his brother that justice will be served no matter who might be involved:

> Si a la enmienda
> vuestro amor no se apercibe,
> dejando vanos intentos
> de bellezas imposibles,
> donde el alma de un vasallo
> con ley soberana vive,
> podrá ser de mi justicia
> que aun mi sangre no se libre.†[10]

But when Don Pedro asks his brother to identify the dagger that Gutierre has found in his wife's bedroom, the prince "accidentally" wounds the king with the weapon, and the king's judicial efforts disintegrate into a spasm of fear and foreboding. The therapeutic effect of law has been weakened; and Gutierre, privately, must become the physician of his own honor; he must take it upon himself to denature the upheaval.[11]

The protagonist, Gutierre, is the only character in *El médico de su honra* who responds successfully to the prince. His reaction entails the suppression of a private emotion, jealousy, and a dedication to the task of scientific purgation of self, family, and society. Calderón does not suppress Gutierre's jealousy altogether, rather he presents it as a real and dangerous passion that may at any time emerge in his consciousness and that, through Gutierre's efforts to tame it, indicates Gu-

10. Ibid., p. 340.
11. For a discussion of the king's weakness and how it affects what Gutierre must do, and for a convincing treatment of other points important to an understanding of the play, see Frank P. Casa, "Crime and Responsibility in *El médico de su honra*."

tierre's dedication to task. When Gutierre becomes aware of his own jealousy he tries to stifle it. The defense of honor requires rational behavior. Gutierre himself says as much in his first monologue on the subject of honor, in which the word *celos* slips out as if by accident:

> Gutierre: . . . ¿Celos dije? ¿Celos dije?
> Pues basta; que cuando llega
> un marido a saber que hay
> celos, faltará la ciencia;
> y es la cura postrera
> que el médico de honor hacer intenta.†[12]

At the end of the second act Gutierre again slips momentarily into a jealous rage, from which he afterward tries to free himself:

> Gutierre: . . . ¿Celoso? ¿Sabes tú lo que son celos?
> Que yo no sé qué son, ¡viven los cielos!
> porque si lo supiera,
> y celos. . . .
> Mencía (ap[arte]): ¡Ay de mí!
> Gutierre: . . . llegar pudiera
> a tener . . . ¿qué son celos?
> Átomos, ilusiones y desvelos,
> no más que de una esclava, una criada,
> por sombra imaginada,
> con hechos iluminados
> a pedazos sacara con mis manos
> el corazón, y luego,
> envuelto en sangre, desatado en fuego,
> el corazón comiera
> a bocados, la sangre me bebiera
> el alma le sacara,
> y el alma, ¡vive Dios!, despedazara,
> si capaz de dolor el alma fuera.
> Pero ¿cómo hablo yo desta manera?
> Mencía: Temor al alma ofreces.
> Gutierre: ¡Jesús!, ¡Jesús mil veces!
> ¡Mi bien, mi esposa, cielo, gloria mía!
> ¡Ah mi dueño! Ah, Mencía!

12. Calderón, *El médico de su honra*, p. 335.

> Perdona, por tus ojos,
> esta descompostura, estos enojos;
> que tanto un fingimiento
> fuera de mí llevó mi pensamiento:
> y vete, por tu vida; que prometo
> que te miro con miedo y con respeto
> corrido de este exceso.
> ¡Jesús! No estuve en mí, no tuve seso.
>
> Mencía (ap.): Miedo, espanto, temor y horror tan fuerte
> parasismos han sido de mi muerte.
>
> Gutierre (ap.): Pues médico me llamo de mi honra,
> yo cubriré con tierra mi deshonra.†[13]

Gutierre's outburst is, in his own eyes, an "exceso," a danger-ous reversion to passionate feeling. Mencía also so regards it, and in it she sees her own death. If Calderón had had Gutierre kill Mencía in a jealous rage, his play would escape the charge of coldness, which is best expressed by Valle-Inclán in the char-acter of Don Estrafalario in *Los cuernos de Don Friolera*:

> "Shakespeare es violento, pero no dogmático. La crueldad española tiene toda la bárbara liturgia de los Autos da Fe. Es fría y antipática . . . es una furia escolástica . . . tiene toda la antipatía de los códigos, desde la Constitución a la Gramática."[14]

But Gutierre suppresses his jealousy to assume the role of the coolheaded physician, a transformation apparent in the scene excerpted above; and he kills his wife, as it were, in cold blood and by proxy. Mencía foresees her death, however, not in the cool dissimulating husband, but in the enraged monster whose emotional control has momentarily slipped. Is she wrong in her inference, or is the rational "médico" an unreal figure su-perimposed upon an enraged and violent husband? And is the bloodletting more intense because the jealous passion has been repressed? Calderón is everywhere an upholder of "grammars" and "constitutions," of social restraints on, and repressions of,

---

13. Ibid., p. 338.
14. "Shakespeare is violent, but not dogmatic. Spanish cruelty has all the barbarous liturgy of the Autos da Fe. It's cold and repellent . . . it's a scholastic fury . . . it has the repulsiveness of all codes, from constitu-tions to grammars." Ramón del Valle-Inclán, *Los cuernos de Don Friolera*, in *Martes de carnaval* (Madrid: Espasa-Calpe, 1973), p. 73.

"instinctual" behavior; yet in this play the agent of repression is so violent in his feelings, and so cold in his appearance and actions, that he is difficult to accept as exemplary of anything good. He is a man alienated from himself, and it is hard to believe that Calderón could create such a character without some detachment and implied criticism.

Although Gutierre's surgical bloodletting has shown, in a contained form, the violence of a bloody vengeance, it is still true that he has solved a problem that has been beyond the power of either Mencía or the king to solve. He has eliminated one of the sources of trouble: his wife. He has done so secretly, and so protected both his reputation and that of the king, whose inability to curb his brother is thus excused, since the brother's involvement has been kept from public knowledge. That Mencía has been in a technical sense innocent, and that Gutierre's means of getting rid of her has been in every sense extreme, is apparent. Even the king, whose work has been done for him at another's cost, is shocked. He asks Gutierre to explain himself, which Gutierre does through a series of questions:

> Gutierre: ¿Si vuelvo a verme
> en desdichas tan extrañas,
> que de noche halle embozado
> a vuestro hermano en mi casa . . . ?
> Rey: No dar crédito a sospechas.
> Gutierre: ¿Yi si detrás de mi cama
> hallase tal vez, señor,
> de Don Enrique la daga?
> Rey: Presumir que hay en el mundo
> mil sobornadas criadas
> y apelar a la cordura.
> Gutierre: A veces, señor, no basta.
> ¿Si veo rondar después
> de noche y de día mi casa?
> Rey: Quejárseme a mí.
> Gutierre: ¿Y si cuando
> llego a quejarme, me aguarda
> mayor desdicha escuchando?
> Rey: ¿Que importa, si él desengaña,
> que fue siempre su hermosura

                    una constante muralla
                    de los vientos defendida?
     Gutierre: ¿Y si volviendo a mi casa
                    hallo algún papel que pide
                    que el infante no se vaya?
        Rey: Para todo habrá remedio,
     Gutierre: ¿Posible es que a esto le haya?
        Rey: Sí, Gutierre.
     Gutierre: ¿Cuál, señor?
        Rey: Uno vuestro.
     Gutierre: ¿Qué es?
        Rey: Sangrarla.†[15]

The king thus approves and excuses Gutierre's action as having
been forced upon him by the circumstances of Mencía's guilty
behavior and the king's own inability to do justice. Gutierre
professes to have suffered:

     Gutierre: . . . Vuelve a esta parte la cara,
                    y verás sangriento el sol,
                    verás la luna eclipsada,
                    deslucidas las estrellas
                    y las esferas borradas;
                    y verás a la hermosura
                    más triste y más desdichada,
                    que por darme mayor muerte,
                    no me ha dejado sin alma.†[16]

It might be thought, because he ordered his wife's death, that
his expression of pain afterward is hypocritical. He does not
admit responsibility, but rather sees himself as a victim of
circumstances. But it seems, in the context given him by Calderón, that it is precisely as a victim that he is to be regarded.
Gutierre has acted out of necessity and against his own feelings, or some of them. He is to be pitied as a bereaved husband and as a victim of the force of opinion; he is to be admired
(with a shocked *admiración*) as a successful and ingenious
strategist. If Calderón had presented the action of the play
to his audience as completely successful and happy, he would
deserve the antipathy shown him by Menéndez Pelayo,

15. Calderón, *El médico de su honra*, p. 348.
16. Ibid.

Valle-Inclán et al.; but the play is not a celebration of Gutierre's unhappily necessary and desperate behavior, nor is it a defense of the honor values as such. It is an enactment of the devastation that instinctual behavior brings and of the price that must be paid if such behavior is to be controlled.

To the play's central problem of discovering a way to control nature, Calderón finds a solution: a dedication to order so unswerving that it compensates for the inaction of a vacillating and doomed monarch, suppresses personal feelings, and separates the agent of control from his emotions. To a subsidiary question—Why is that control necessary?—Calderón does not provide an answer, he merely takes for granted that it is. Gutierre must act as he does because his honor is his life; his reputation is his existence. It is not fanciful to see in Gutierre's predicament a reflection of the struggle to maintain the appearance of *limpieza de sangre*, which Castro regards as an essential feature of the Spanish society of Calderón's time. Castro argues persuasively that this analogy is implicit in the honor plays of Lope de Vega:

> En la vida diaria—no en la vivida en las comedias de Lope de Vega—, el drama atroz surgía cuando un español se daba cuenta de que no era tenido por cristiano viejo, es decir, por miembro de la casta dominante, y que su hombría no le servía para nada. Pero este drama sordo y oprimente no fue llevado a la escena, no era posible hacerlo. Tomar distancia escénica respecto a él hubiera exigido que la sociedad española no fuese como en efecto era, o sea, que en ella hubiera sido factible situarse fuera de su ámbito, y contemplarla críticamente y desde arriba en el teatro. Esperar nada así en la España del siglo XVI sería tan anacrónico como absurdo.

In an important footnote, Castro adds:

> Pero Lope de Vega representó el violento conflicto entre las "razones" individuales del amor y las sociales de la henra en *El castigo sin venganza*.[17]

17. "In daily life, not in the life lived in the plays of Lope de Vega, the atrocious drama arose whenever a Spaniard found out that he was not being taken for an Old Christian, that is, for a member of the dominant caste, and that his manhood was of no use to him. But this mute and oppressive drama was not put on stage; it was impossible to do so. To assume aesthetic distance with regard to it would have required that

In *El médico de su honra*, there is a conflict between private emotion and social necessity in which social necessity wins out, perhaps in a manner paralleling, as Castro would maintain, the need to maintain the appearance of *limpieza* in daily life. With Calderón there is, in addition, a deeply held psychosexual necessity, a need to combat and repress the sexuality that throughout his plays is a sower of confusion and a source of disorder. It is the subjection of the passions, and not the so-called honor code (Calderón's attitude toward which has been fruitlessly debated by his defenders and detractors), that is the play's main concern. *El médico de su honra* may be coherent even to one who does not know, and does not care, about what honor meant to a seventeenth-century Spaniard.

*   *   *   *   *

At the moment of Gutierre's greatest success, the peace he has achieved is marred by images of horror. His rational persona as the surgeon of his own honor draws some of its power from the violent personality it surmounts. The killing of Mencía, which seems to be a considered and secret act, is really an open act of repressed violence—shocking in itself and made public by way of the blood that overwhelms the play near the end of the third act. The king, who approves Gutierre's secret vengeance and marries him again, to Leonor, is a doomed monarch, his justice no more binding than his ability to rule effectively. Gutierre's remarriage is itself of dubious prospects; he has left Leonor before for fear that she will dishonor him—might he not do so again?

The language of *El médico de su honra*, so masterful in its rhetorical control, is at the same time hyperbolic and melodramatic. What it finally attains through its tense resolution of opposites is a despairing apprehension of violence, dangerous eroticism, and emotionalism so strong that it seems to corrupt even the forces that seek to suppress it. Calderón is the witness

---

Spanish society be other than the way it was, and that while within it it might have been possible to situate oneself at the same time outside its orbit to contemplate it critically, from above, in the theater. To expect anything like that in the Spain of the sixteenth century would be as anachronistic as it is absurd. . . . But Lope de Vega enacted the conflict between the individual motives of love and the social ones of honor in *El castigo sin venganza*." Castro, *De la edad conflictiva*, p. 34.

to what happens when repression is a way of life. He spares and omits very little. His is a true vision of a distorted world, a vision not of a critical outsider but of an insider percipient enough to expose the pain that living in such a world can bring.

El alcalde de Zalamea

Among the most admired plays of the Spanish Golden Age are the peasant honor dramas, which are cast in the mold perfected by Lope de Vega. Calderón's *El alcalde de Zalamea*[1] falls within this category, along with such works as Lope's *El mejor alcalde, el rey; Fuenteovejuna;* and *Peribáñez y el comendador de Ocaña. El alcalde,* alone among Calderón's plays, has been praised even by those readers who, while proclaiming Lope's genius, have rejected nearly all of Calderón's work as artificial, labored, and unwholesome. The reasons for this popularity are not hard to find. Calderón's language, although never "natural," is here subtle and differentiated according to the author's intention and the character types; it encompasses the slang of the camp followers, Isabel's tortured gongoresque lament, Don Mendo's empty chivalresque rhetoric, Crespo's dignified affirmation of self and law, and the rough, candid tones of Don Lope de Figueroa. The play has a memorable and enigmatic main character. It can be regarded, by one so inclined, as a tempered protest against military authority—with a hint of revolution.[2] Most appealing of all is its treatment of honor. Here at last, it seems, is a play in which

1. Pedro Calderón de la Barca, *El alcalde de Zalamea*, in *Obras completas*, 5th ed., vol. 1, ed. A. Valbuena Briones (Madrid: Aguilar, 1966), p. 535.

2. Especially interesting is the comment of the German-American film director Douglas Sirk: "*El alcalde de Zalamea*, by Calderón [is] interesting in two ways as far as my picture making is concerned: as a very popular play and as a piece of tremendous social criticism—Catholicism can be a means of social criticism, too. *El alcalde de Zalamea* is a play of the utmost audacity, certainly for its time, if not for any. The play runs its uncompromising way down to the end, or almost to it; then, in order to achieve the necessary happy outcome of the goings on, when there is apparently no way out, God steps forward in the person of the king and ties up all the threads, punishes the bad, and pardons the good one, who is the revolutionary. This is done in the crude shocking manner

"honor," whatever else others may think it to be, is affirmed by the play's hero only as it upholds human dignity and law; it is not an inherited and mechanically invoked class possession.

Like all of Calderón's plays, *El alcalde de Zalamea* projects an intensified vision of the human emotions and of the means necessary to govern them. The presentation, typically, is colored by a view of the instinctual that causes the characters' impulses to reveal themselves in ways magically transformed from the "natural" to the figurative. Calderón works in an intellectual but violent allegory of what he seems to fear the emotions to be; the plot of *El alcalde de Zalamea* deals with a response to a melodramatically brutal act, a rape. The effects of this assault can never be erased completely. Isabel, although not sacrificed, is confined to a convent; Crespo's loss abides. Never in his secular plays does Calderón rid his world of evil and its consequences, although some kind of valid order can be restored through an effort of will directed against a hostile world. In affirming an order, Crespo must use his ingenuity to combat the captain's contempt, Don Lope's legally correct but narrow claim of exclusive jurisdiction, Juan's lust for revenge, and, not the least, his own concealed but ever-present pride of reputation, which, if it had not been redeemed through the lucky discovery of its congruence with a higher law, might itself have degenerated into revenge. He is equal to the task, but no matter how necessary Crespo's justice may be to the safeguarding of civilized behavior, it is achieved through sleight of hand and it freezes (in a convergence of law and vengeance) the conflicts it attempts to put to rest.

To say that Crespo's justice is also his vengeance is not to say that he acts hypocritically when he falls to his knees to beg the captain to marry Isabel or that his arguments with Don Lope over the legality of his jurisdiction are merely self-serving. There is room for doubt here, however: Isabel, when left unpunished after her "dishonoring" (spared by her father from a punishment her brother really means to carry out), is not sure whether Crespo's mercy derives from his craft in guarding his reputation or his wisdom in seeking a more morally appropriate redress:

of Euripides. It is the perfect pattern for a melodrama." Jon Halliday, ed., *Sirk on Sirk* (New York: Viking, 1972), p. 70.

Isabel (ap.):   Fortuna mía,
        o mucha cordura, o mucha
        cautela es esta.†[3]

Crespo's act of jailing his own son along with the captain serves more than one purpose. It protects both Juan and Isabel, and it gives the appearance of evenhandedness to his justice. His execution of the captain before receiving authorization betrays a determination to take the law into his own hands. Yet the ends, finally, do justify the means; Crespo's actions are just, and the king approves them after the fact.

The terms of Crespo's response, however, partake of the insult-vengeance honor complex. As a consequence, they are impure; for in Calderón's treatment, as the honor plays show, vengeance is the obverse of insult, and the defense of honor is a response to a personal threat. There is some reason to believe that Don Lope is right in maintaining that Crespo has exceeded his jurisdiction and that his pious rectitude masks a successful effort at revenge. If Crespo's defense is to be favored over the law's jurisdiction, a higher authority must be called in; thus the king intervenes. It is an intervention as arbitrary as Calderón's forced equation of honor with divine right (patrimonio del alma); the effect is finally to seal the dispute in a dynamic equilibrium that keeps the initial terms unchanged. Where honor is threatened it must be defended, and if the defense at times requires exceptions to the letter of the law, it must be justified by royal authority.

El alcalde de Zalamea enacts a sexual theme, but one caught up in the honor action. A heightened perception of instinctual sexuality takes the shape of a violent threat to honor; and excessive reaction—the overkill of conscience—shows itself in Crespo's willful self-defense. It is as if Calderón's representation of the emotions were a conflict in which the only actors are the id and the superego, while the poor ego is submerged and battered. The honor action is suited for the depiction of such a struggle, but it can lead to none but a forced resolution. Since the terms of the conflict are so limited, one side must be

† This symbol indicates that an English translation is given in the Appendix, pp. 106–22.

3. Calderón, *El alcalde de Zalamea*, p. 563.

imposed upon the other: conscience overcomes license, honor defeats dishonor. But in its reimposition the victorious idea reasserts the values that have nurtured its antagonist. It is honor, after all, that lies behind the arrogance of the military state, Don Mendo's callous desire to exploit, and the captain's refusal to marry beneath himself. As Crespo obtains honor he joins them. It is Calderón's fear of the erotic that colors and limits his attitude toward love and causes him to taint an otherwise sympathetic character by giving him an ignobly defensive craft. This fear is so strong that it makes impossible the depiction of sexual love in any but the grossest terms and, in sharp contrast to Lope de Vega, excludes lyricism from the play. The soldiers' and camp followers' serenade in act 2 is recognizably gongoresque, but in its context it is sinister:

> Las flores del romero,
> niña Isabel,
> hoy son flores azules,
> mañana serán miel†[4]

When Lope occasionally adds music to the actions of one of his evil characters (as in the song "Al val de Fuenteovejuna/ la niña en cabellos baja" in *Fuenteovejuna*) he suspends his moral judgment temporarily to extract the impersonal beauty of the situation. Calderón undermines the song's beauty, or at least its innocence.

Lope de Vega, whose essential effort is to rediscover the instinctual, finally achieves a natural harmony in his work. But Lope's order is more stable than Calderón's because it develops from an attempt to achieve positive identification with primary experience; and, when an ordered end is possible, it is through the elaboration of those impulses that Calderón tries so hard to contain.

Lope's affective model is the *romancero*, with its "naive" exposition of the natural world that is forever attractive to the sophisticate who, like Lope and unlike Calderón, is aware of, and sorry for, his separation from a world of uncomplicated emotional experience. In entering that world, Lope leads him-

4. Ibid., p. 553.

self and his audience back into contact with the joy of guiltless sexual love. In *Peribáñez*, the innocent sexuality of Peribáñez and Casilda and its affinity to a utopian and pastoral nature, as well as to affective religion, are apparent:

> Casilada: . . . Acabada la comida,
> puestas las manos los dos,
> dámosle gracias a Dios
> por la merced recibida;
> y vámonos a acostar,
> donde le pesa la aurora
> cuando se llega la hora
> de venirnos a llamar.†[5]

This innocence is, however, the ideal of a sophisticate, as is made evident by the fact that Lope invests the play's most important character, the *comendador*, with an awareness of his own estrangement from Peribáñez's simple delights. The *comendador* is a civilized man, with a civilized man's sense of guilt. What Peribáñez, in his Edenic state, enjoys naturally becomes, in the *comendador*'s imagination and aborted attempt at seizure, an impossibility—self-conscious, forbidden, finally fatal.

There is a superficial similarity in the dramatic functions of Lope's *comendador* and Calderón's captain. Each is a nobleman; each has sexual designs upon a peasant woman; each meets his death at the hands of a peasant whose newly won honor he has offended. But Calderón's captain has no shame, nor even any redeeming respect for the object of his desire; he is unreflectively brutal and cynical. Lope's *comendador*, in contrast, knows all too well the worm of conscience. His desire for Casilda is a desire to experience vicariously what he knows to be innocent. His love is less a slavish obedience to passion than an impossible wish to enjoy it. The *comendador*'s attempt to supplant Peribáñez, to take his place as a pure lover, is a futile effort to gain a form of experience denied him by his civilized scruple, which tells him that what he wants is good but that his wanting it is not. He finally acquiesces in his own destruction out of obedience to a supercivilized perception of what he can never, because of his very capacity to desire and

5. Lope de Vega, *Peribáñez*, act 1, scene 13, lines 755–61.

envy it, enjoy for himself. His conscience, and his self-chosen identification with Peribáñez's paradisiacal, natural innocence ("¿Estás contento, Peribáñez?"), make the *comendador* a sympathetic figure; his death, in a way that borders on the sacramental, insures the continuance of Peribáñez's love and of all that it represents.

It is a commonplace, and a true one (as far as it goes), that the *comedia*—the theater of Calderón as well as that of Lope and his followers—serves a set of national attitudes: a belief in the greatness and destiny of the Spanish realm, in the truth of the Catholic religion, in the common blood (free of Semitic taint) of the Spanish people, in the power of faith, and in the importance of honor. Both *Peribáñez* and *El alcalde de Zalamea* have a format suitable to the affirmation of such abstractions. Yet the two plays are not very alike. The axiological limits beyond which the *comedia* does not stray serve as the given facts of a well-defined state of civilization; but Lope's attitude toward civilization is different from Calderón's, and the use to which each playwright puts his society's most dearly held tenets in each case furthers a private vision all the more coherent for its clear relationship to a fixed ideological system with which it does not at all times coincide. In *Arte nuevo*, Lope admits to some detachment from his honor plays; he says that they are good because they move people "con fuerza." This connotes a willingness to provide the expected, as well as a need to claim some distance. It is not altogether accidental that some of the Spanish national values serve Lope well—especially the idea of a polity united in faith, purpose, and blood. From this myth, Lope creates his own imaginary paradise, but it would be wrong to assume that Lope is unaware that the myth is real only in his theater. Calderón, if less detached, is, if anything, more ambivalent than Lope in his attitude toward some of his society's habits and institutions. His ambivalence toward authority and the determinism of the honor situation is so apparent that it has engendered whole theories based upon the incomplete premise that he is antiauthoritarian and hostile to conformist pressures. In fact, Calderón does concentrate upon the points at which institutions and beliefs approach a breakdown, but he invariably shores them up with eschatology or reaction.

Lope's "unreal" apotheosis of the Spanish myth of social

and racial purity and of Calderón's tense rearguard struggle to defend its real and reified social premises deserve to be taken seriously. One should resist the temptation to condemn Lope for his dreamy flights from reality, or Calderón for his inability to reach good answers to the problems he perceives and documents. Such criticism may be left to the implied message of Cervantes. Lope's utopia and Calderón's civilization reflect the playwrights' attempts to deal with the problem of alienation in a civilized value system that must be upheld against time and history and alienation itself.

In neither *Peribáñez* nor *El alcalde de Zalamea* is the essential problem the protagonist's alienation from society; rather it is his society's alienation from him. Peribáñez and Pedro Crespo, and the idealized rural worlds they inhabit, are the standards against which the inevitable deviation and corruption of history may be measured and unfavorably compared. The simple peasant heroes, with their incorruptible virtues and their untainted purity of blood, act to defend the integrity of self and ideal against the attack of a representative of a greater society that has degenerated through the pursuit of the nonessential and the nonpastoral: class (as opposed to caste) privilege, urbanity, luxury, separation from the earth. It is the society outside the rural paradise that must be reformed, the alienation of the outer world from the infrasociety must be bridged. This is not easy, however, because that alienation results from the inevitable separations and divisions of labor that any large social organization requires; and the original values to which the peasant hero, through exemplary action, must rededicate the entire nation are precisely those that have generated the abuses and conflicts that the plays attempt to put to rest.

Peribáñez's place as a *labrador* presupposes the existence of a *comendador* to defend him; the *comendador*'s status as a man separated from Peribáñez's natural enjoyments results inevitably from his position as a member of a "warrior" class, from which stem also his special consciousness and his special needs. Even the *comendador*'s sexual desire, which seems so guilty and devious when compared to Peribáñez's guiltless love, can be seen as the inevitable nostalgia for nature that accompanies any disassociation caused by awareness of artifice. The situation in *El alcalde* is similar to that in *Peribáñez* in this respect: Crespo depends upon the very soldiery that oppresses him to secure the continuance of his world. To maintain the army, the king, and the state, Crespo will sacrifice his wealth and even his son; but he will not renounce his honor, his prime attribute, which he possesses as a prototypical *cristiano viejo*. But honor is the value that has produced the perversions from which Crespo suffers: Don Mendo's idiotic vanity, the captain's scorn, the military's arrogance.

To affirm and reestablish the national value system while at the same time denying, or renouncing, what it must produce as it evolves, is as much as to perceive a contradiction and to attempt, in a poetic vision, to surmount the formal-logical laws of contradiction. This is the business of poets and dialecticians. It must be accepted that Lope is better than Calderón at both poetry and dialectics, but that does not mean that Lope is a more interesting writer. Lope is the romantic; like Schiller and Herder, like Hegel and Marx, Lope envisions the history of mankind as a process of restoring the unity of man with himself and with nature—a unity that has been lost as man's power of differentiation and antagonism (alienation) has developed. The final harmony achieved is on a higher level than the undifferentiated primal unity, and this final vision of harmony itself celebrates and justifies the very differentiated vision without which there can be no understanding of what unity is. Lope's play begins in a unity cemented by Eros, proceeds through a dialectic between love and death that expresses forms of dying within life (consciousness, guilt, alienation, differentiation), and ends with the tragicomic unity of life and death. Consciousness dies willingly so that what only consciousness can fully perceive may live, eternally. Calderón, the antiromantic, accepts differentiation and alienation as unalterable facts. His play begins and ends in an unresolved struggle that he attempts to resolve forcibly through the invocation of law, his provision against the intuition that there may be no natural harmony at all. The ideal order to Calderón is the civilized order, as can be inferred, for example, from Pedro Crespo's description of his estate:

> esta tarde
> salí a mirar la labranza,
> y están las parvas notables

de manojos y montones,
que parecen, al mirarse
desde lejos, montes de oro,
y aun oro de más quilates,
pues de los granos de aqueste
es todo el cielo el contraste.
Allí el bielgo, hiriendo a soplos
el viento en ellos süave,
deja en esta parte el grano
y la paja en la otra parte;
que aun allí lo más humilde
da el lugar a lo más grave.
¡Oh, quiera Dios que en las trojes
yo llegue a encerrarlo, antes
que algún turbión me lo lleve
o algún viento me lo tale!†[6]

This passage is absolutely complete and sure in its correspondence with the manner of life it reflects—a life, like an
art, in which the most usable of what the world offers is to be
harvested (and the rest discarded), in which what is harvested
becomes gold, to be displayed in its laboriously worked perfection and guarded always against an intensely perceived
threat of irrational destruction. The "turbión," or the apprehension of it, is the price that Crespo, and Calderón, and all of
us, must pay for an artificial victory over nature and, one is
tempted to say, over the unconscious. Calderón knows the
price, and he argues that it must always be paid. History does
not change anything; there is no going back and there is no
going forward, there is only the repeated necessity to reaffirm
the law that accommodates Segismundo, upholds Crespo, justifies Fernando, and, with all generosity, appears from above
to save "el hombre," that is, everyone, from his anxiety by
offering the promise of a better life beyond time and space.

6. Calderón, *El alcalde de Zalamea*, p. 544.

Eco y Narciso

There is no better way for a reader to find out whether, in spite of everything, he really likes Calderón than for him to read a few of the mythological plays, the *fêtes galantes* Calderón composed for the entertainment of the royal family toward the end of his career and at the very end of Spain's century and a half of political presumption and literary greatness. These musical dramas are the merest and purest artifice; they elevate artifice itself into its own subject. Lacking any serious mimetic or intellectual substance, they have no religious, moral, political, social, or metaphysical content; they have only a style. To the person who dislikes this style, none of Calderón's work will finally mean very much; he who does like it will like it wherever he finds it, but perhaps he will like it most of all in those plays in which no important values are introduced or undermined.

There never was a manner without its own meaning, however; and in Calderón's mythological dramas an entire vision of the world is conveyed by fancy language, decorative splendor, arch mummery, and amused, skeptical aestheticizing. To write in such a way Calderón must have made a facile but not completely deplorable first assumption: that there are no new intuitions to be made about reality and that therefore one might as well play with words. Such an attitude may be said to project a baroque anxiety concerning the reality of the natural world, and so it is somehow almost inevitable that Calderón should finally have come to find delight and inspiration in Ovidian transformations, from which he could easily create spectacles of evanescence.

The greatest shortcoming of Calderón's theater is its attempt to encompass the infinite through the manipulation of finite elements of plot, language, and thought. This makes his plays seem both sensationalistic and scholastic, which they are, but only in part. They also embody a strong, admirable, but un-

successful effort to control the mutable elements of a reality
that is never completely ignored and that is intuited in an in-
terestingly lurid form. Still, the truth of Calderón's effort does
not completely obscure the limitations of his themes and conclusions. It is not hard to understand James Joyce's disgust
with the admiration his bourgeois contemporaries bestowed
upon the reified spirituality of that baroque mode from which
Calderón's art cannot be separated:

> Many, whose palates have grown accustomed to the old food,
> cry out peevishly against a change of diet. To these use and want
> is the seventh heaven. Loud are their praises of the bland
> blatancy of Corneille, the starchglazing of Trapassi's godliness,
> the Pumblechookian woodenness of Calderón. Their infantile
> plot juggling sets them agape, so superfine it is.[1]

If such charges can justly be brought against Calderón's
comedias, and they can, then who should bother to defend his
mythological dramas? These fluffy operettas can boast of nothing but superfine talk and infantile plot juggling; they retain
barely a vestige of whatever truth the *comedia* told the Spanish
nation about itself. Yet neither do they confuse truth with
artifice. They do not pretend to be transcendental, and so they
escape a certain kind of censure. It may be true that Calderón's
"serious" *comedias*, even with their occasional overreaching,
are more interesting and important than are his mythological
plays (this conclusion is almost inevitable); yet still these last
plays are delicacies.

*   *   *   *   *

In his *Eco y Narciso*,[2] Calderón alters Ovid's story in a
number of unimportant ways, as well as in one very important
way: for the prophecy of Ovid's Tiresias—in which the sage
tells Liriope that Narcissus will live to an old age only if he
never comes to know himself ("Si se non noverit")—Calderón substitutes something different:

1. James Joyce, "Drama and Life," in *The Critical Writings of James
Joyce*, ed. Ellsworth Mason and Richard Ellman (New York: Viking
Press, 1959).
2. Pedro Calderón de la Barca, *Eco y Narciso*, ed. Charles V. Aubrun
(Paris: Publications du Centre de Recherches d'Études Hispaniques,
1963).

Encinta estás. Un garzón
Bellísimo has de parir.
Una voz y una hermosura
Solicitarán su fin,
Amando y aborreciendo.
Guárdale de ver y oír.†[3]

Since the action in both Ovid and Calderón is meant to work
itself out in such a way as to sustain these prophecies, it follows that the differing predictions will lead to different events,
and in that sense Calderón's alteration (like his other less
important ones) can be said to be justified as a matter of adap-
tation. A fable must be changed to be made into a play. But
the change is great enough to call for a closer examination,
which might reveal something about the requirements of Cal-
deron's theater and the import of his apparently "incorrect"
reading of Ovid.

Although we do not know exactly what Ovid's Tiresias
understands self-knowledge to be, we do know more or less
the way in which his Narcissus comes to know himself. Narcissus sees his own reflection, and to him the reflection becomes
the world; he is a solipsist. He is also a narcissist in that he
does not just fall in love with his image, but he also wants his
image to return his pathetically projected self-love. It is this
desire that kills him. It is an irony that Ovid in his fable seems
to confuse this syndrome with self-knowledge.

In Calderón's play, the prediction of Tiresias does not mention self-knowledge, rather it warns against the fatal effects
of two external stimuli, *una voz y una hermosura*. Líríope in-
terprets the warning (especially the final admonition: *guárdale
de ver y oír*) to mean that she should keep Narciso away from
all contact with others, which she tries to do. It does not work;
and the irony, no surprise to anyone familiar with Ovid's fable,
is that Narciso's own reflection is the *hermosura* his mother
was warned against. (The *voz*, that is, Eco, involves a superfluous but telling mannerism of plot that enables Calderón's
Echo, unlike Ovid's, to become involved as a manipulating
agent.) What matters here, however, is that when Narciso sees

† This symbol indicates that an English translation is given in the
Appendix, pp. 106–22.
3. Ibid., p. 19.

his image he does not see a projection of his "self," he does not
approach self-knowledge. He sees an image, a *figura*, a decep-
tive surface, an illusion; and when he sees it he does not want
it to love him, he wants it to give itself up to his possession.
For Calderón, understanding comes with the realization that
the pursuit of beauty and pleasure is a vain one; and he bends
Ovid's fable in order to make this point.

Narciso wants to possess his image even after he is told
that it is an unattainable illusion, he persists even after he has
caído en la cuenta.

> Porque, al ir (¡hay pena igual!)
> A asirla, de amores loco,
> su luz turbó celestial;
> y yo sólo el cristal toco
> y no el alma del cristal.†[4]

There is nothing particularly childlike in this headlong and
despairing pursuit of beauty; on the contrary, it is a full-blown
adult substitution of an object (the image) for a need (the
need to be loved). Everywhere Calderón makes the point that
beautiful objects do not suffice, that we die in the pursuit of
"el alma del cristal," that spirit and matter are divorced beyond
reconciliation. Ovid seems to say that we project ourselves and
our needs upon the world; Calderón tells us that the world
deceives us.

In this play, though, unlike some others we have been reading, Calderón seems to laugh at himself; so he wins an instan-
taneous reprieve. It is satisfying to be given a picture of a
dreamlike, unstable world and yet not be forced to accept the
Church, the state, or some other rigid finitude as the only de-
pendable order. Of course, *Eco y Narciso* ends with the invocation of an eternal mythical order, but this is done through
a very artificial deus ex machina stage trick; it is a bagatelle,
and meant to be taken as such. As one of the characters says
at the end of the play: *Habrá bobos que lo crean*. Although
we may not believe in these events any more than he says we
should, we may still be inclined, at times, to see the world as
though it were a hallucination and to feel deceived by its
beauty, which can never quite be possessed. The temptation

4. Ibid., p. 57.

to revel in beautiful objects is a general one, not confined to Calderón, his characters, or his audience. To do so, to know that one is doing so, to know that it cannot satisfy, and yet to do it anyway, is perhaps to be a decadent. *Eco y Narciso* may be said to be a decadent play about decadence, but it does not pretend to be anything else; and whatever it is not, it is a beautiful verbal object, rich with the literary decoration of the century that preceded it.

9

Language

Calderón's language is first of all correct. Second, it is not obscure. It may be difficult and involved, strained and stretched, but a sentence of Calderón's, no matter how involuted and boggling, can be pressed into a straight line. Lope's work, in contrast, has some anacolutha; his language is also richer in ambiguities than Calderón's. It would be foolish to suggest that Calderón's good grammar is itself an impoverishment, but it may be said that Calderón's grammatical control serves an imagination so strongly in the service of primary colors that even the occasional nuance of impreciseness is foreign to it. Calderón's dramatic vocabulary, his words, images, plots, and characters, all derive from the *comedia*; yet his drama is in some ways antithetical to much of the *comedia*. Likewise, the way he arranges his verbal material, although it may seem to be merely a process of careful and considered ordering of an inherited language, is in fact, because of its manifest passion for symmetry and order, the act of creating a new language.

These statements, which are implicit everywhere in this study, may be illustrated with reference to specific passages such as the following (quoted earlier) from early in the first act of *El médico de su honra*, when Mencía reacts to Enrique's fall:

> Venía
> un bizarro caballero
> en un bruto tan ligero,
> que en el viento parecía
> un pájaro que volaba;
> y es razón que lo presumas
> porque un penacho de plumas
> matices al aire daba.
> El campo y el sol en ellas
> compitieron resplandores;

que el campo le dio sus flores,
y el sol le dio sus estrellas;
porque cambiaban de modo,
y de modo relucían,
que en todo al sol parecían,
y a la primavera en todo.
Corrió, pues, y tropezó
el caballo, de manera
que lo que ave entonces era
cuando en la tierra cayó
fue rosa; y así en rigor
imitó su lucimiento
en sol, cielo, tierra y viento
ave, bruto, estrella y flor.†[1]

The symbols, or images, employed by Calderón in this speech are firmly fixed in his inherited language and characteristic of the *comedia*. What is interesting in this speech is Calderón's proportional and orderly presentation of the symbols. The metaphors can be placed in equations, such as $A:x::B:y$, or caballero: bruto:: plumas:aire::pájaro:viento, and so forth. *Caballero* and *pájaro* have very little in common intrinsically; they are not linked by contiguity, or even, really, by analogy (although this could be argued). What connects them in this speech is the similarity of the effects that they might have upon an observer. Since the speaker, Mencía, has just observed something important, the speech is suited to her condition as an agitated witness; but the actual rhetoric of the speech is far from uncertain or tremulous, it is dominating and assured. Mencía does not see in an ordinary "human" way, nor does she speak as people speak outside of Calderonian dramas. Her vision and her speech have been refined by the playwright into something that approximates an effect that has been considered beforehand, one of passive astonishment and fancifully encompassing (though not free) association. The symbols that Calderón has Mencía associate are a kind of metalanguage. They are not seen by her (she sees only a knight fall from a

† This symbol indicates that an English translation is given in the Appendix, pp. 106–22.

1. Pedro Calderón de la Barca, *El médico de su honra*, in *Obras completas*, 5th ed., vol. 1, ed. A. Valbuena Briones (Madrid: Aguilar, 1966), p. 318.

horse); they are not perceived sensually at all, rather they pile up, one upon another, in a conceit that grows arithmetically as additional, preclassified objects are added. These objects form a chain of mutually interrelated *figuras*, which have a relation to the speaker (observer) that is based on *seeming*; the most important verb in the passage is *parecer*. One symbol is in some well-defined way related not to reality but to another symbol that has been reduced, through accepted literary usage and reliance upon intellectualized rather than sensual or particularized imagery, to an essence as schematic as the first symbol. Mencía is the medium through which Calderón sets out these essences; and she is a good one, since her frightened eloquence is characteristic of her creator, much of whose talent lies in his ability to portray an inconstant world through the manipulation of semblances.

A verbal world in which such natural phenomena as the sun and the stars are linked through the ways they are operated upon by the observer's capacity to categorize, a world in which seeing is unsure and thinking is sure, reflects the alienation of its creator's intellect from the natural world. The intellect still has some toys to play with; such as words, ideas, and orderly relationships; with these an artist such as Calderón can construct a finished subworld, pieced together from the fragments of the dramatic language of the *comedia*, which still serve a mimetic purpose but have also been made to enact the playwright's rage for symmetry. Calderón puts these bits together in such a way as to call attention to their arrangement; for this he needs an abundance of "grammar," that is, of verbal tissues (*así en rigor, de manera que, porque, pues, que,* etc.) that ensure order and proper scansion. There is also a visible exoskeleton of parallelisms, brought to an emphatic consummation in the final two lines. The dense poetry of Mencía's speech will be diffused as the play continues, and the symbols it contains will be elaborated on their own; but the expanded pattern never becomes much more than ornamental, and the entire play, for all its beauty, is static.

Lope's *El castigo sin venganza* contains a passage in which speaker and situation resemble those in the passage from Calderón just quoted. Casandra, like Mencía, reacts to a portentous accident: a young man comes upon the scene, and with him will come love and death. Her speech, like Mencía's, introduces images that are developed later as events unfold:

Aun no acierto a encarecer
el haberos conocido:
poco es lo que había oído
para lo que vengo a ver.
El hablar, el proceder
a la persona conforma,
hijo y mi señor, de forma,
que muestra en lo que habéis hecho
cuál es el alma del pecho
que tan gran sujeto informa.
Dicha ha sido haber errado
el camino que seguí,
pues más presto os conocí
por yerro tan acertado.
Cual suele en el mar airado
la tempestad, después della
ver aquella lumbre bella,
así fue mi error la noche,
mar el río, nave el coche,
yo el piloto y vos mi estrella†[2]

There are several reasons Calderón could not have written this, not the least of which is the elation in Casandra's words, which have none of the deathly glitter one finds in the words of Calderón's women. Further, Casandra's speech is not constructed in a Calderonian fashion. There is no attempt to bring every image together in a summation; there almost never is in Lope's work, because his images seem to grow out of one another and do not lend themselves to equation. Since Lope uses fewer equations, he needs much less in the way of grammatical superstructure. It is clear nonetheless what Lope means, because the relationships (mar: río: :nave: coche: :yo: piloto) are metonymically so reasonable that all one has to know is that an accident has occured and that the situation, though confused, may clear up.

2. Lope de Vega, *El castigo sin venganza*, in *Comedias escogidas*, ed. Juan Eugenio Hartzenbusch (Madrid: Biblioteca de Autores Españoles, 1853), p. 571.

There are passages in Lope's plays that are simply ana-
coluthic, such as the following four lines from *El caballero de
Olmedo*:

> Cuanto vive, de amor nace
> y se sustenta de amor;
> cuanto muere, es un rigor
> que nuestras vidas deshace.†[3]

The correct punctuation of this passage is in doubt. Willard F.
King, the play's most recent (and best) editor, gives, in a tex-
tual note, the punctuation of the 1641 edition and that of several subsequent ones. But the problem this passage presents is
not one that punctuation will solve, as the editor points out
when she states that "any of the modern punctuations is possible within the context." In a note on her translation, King
writes: "It is clear that the original text is elliptical and twisted
in its syntax; the intention is reasonably clear—i.e. love both
creates and destroys life—but the words do not fully encompass it."[4]

There are passages in Calderón in which something like
love (or at least desire) has a simultaneously quickening and
killing power, for example this speech by Enrique in *El médico
de su honra*:

> Milagro de su hermosura
> presumí el feliz suceso
> de mi vida, pero ya,
> más desengañado, pienso
> que no fue sino venganza
> de mi muerte; pues es cierto
> que muero, y que no hay milagros
> que se examinen muriendo.†[5]

The grammar here is easy to follow; its only syntactical con-
volution is a single ellipsis. However, the conceit is complicated, even precious. This situation is the opposite of the one
we found in the speech from *El caballero de Olmedo* quoted

3. Lope de Vega, *The Knight of Olmedo (El caballero de Olmedo)*,
trans. and ed. Willard F. King (Lincoln: University of Nebraska Press,
1972), p. 32.
4. Lope de Vega, *The Knight of Olmedo*, p. 178.
5. Calderón, *El médico de su honra*, p. 320.

earlier, where the meaning was fairly clear, even though the language was not. In the passage from Lope, the meaning is carried, as it were, by the rhythm and form of the verse itself, fully as much as by the meaning of the words or their grammatical relationships. *Cuanto vive* and *cuanto muere* are each followed by one and one-half lines of verse; the entire quatrain (which is actually four lines of a décima) is constructed to draw attention to *rigor* and *amor*, the two oxytones, which by virtue of their equal stress acquire meanings that are complementary, as well as contradictory. Something similar occurs with *nace* and *deshace*; they are united by the magnetic surface of Lope's poetry. The passage by Calderón, on the contrary, has the effect of a sentence squeezed into verse. This is not a bad effect; in some ways it is better suited to dramatic poetry than is Lope's lyricism. But it also means that much of the sense has to be carried by an array of conjunctions and dependent clauses, which give this passage a rhythmic choppiness. Rough rhythm, as a correlative of emotional unease is, like good grammar, one of Calderón's trademarks. He doesn't encompass *vida* and *muerte* within a single sweep of language; they remain, as intended, contraries. Calderón's vision is dualistic, and his reigning obsession is to keep control, but his control is no deeper than his ability to get his grammar straight, and it gives life itself, bereft of the unifying power of love, a deathly tinge, just as *vida* and *muerte* are declared equivalent but never reconciled in Enrique's speech.

10

Critics

In this study I have tried to continue a tradition begun by certain men of letters of the nineteenth century who saw in Calderón what I see in him: grandeur and anxiety in a discarnate and timeless imaginary world. I have mentioned the names of these distant mentors here and there along the way: the Schlegels, Shelley, Lewes, Menéndez Pelayo.

In the Schlegels one finds a contagious intuition of magnificence, a conviction that Calderón's art examines a divine scheme and offers a weighty emotion to be shared by the reader. Shelley shared this enthusiasm, but faithful to an English romantic's sense of the natural and concrete (which sometimes, perhaps, eluded him in his own poetry), he faulted Calderón for abstractness and dogmatism. Lewes repeated Shelley's criticism, without the balancing infatuation. Appalled by the Schlegels' favorable comparison of Calderón with Shakespeare, Lewes proved, as if it needed to be proved, that Calderón lacks Shakespeare's gifts of fertile language, subtle characterization, and precise observation. To these he added a moral objection to Calderón's art; he said that it is unreflectively Catholic and bound to destructive social attitudes, which he attributed to time and place. Menéndez Pelayo, presumably on his own, came to all the conclusions drawn by the writers just mentioned; he saw Calderón as a great writer with great weaknesses, the worst of which, in his eyes, was Menéndez Pelayo's own bête noire: affected language and Gongorism. I mention these critics in passing paraphrase because I think that their conclusions are correct and only apparently contradictory. This belief is not shared by the contemporary Calderonians with whose written opinions I am familiar. Far more important to most students of Calderón's theater are the judgments of E. M. Wilson, W. J. Entwistle, and A. A. Parker, the founders of what has been called (perhaps inaccurately, for these critics do not always agree among themselves) the "British school" of Calderón criticism, which has also been called the thematic-structural school.[1] If the reader is familiar with this "school," he has the right to expect me to devote some attention to it. If he is not, he should gain his acquaintance with it firsthand; what I intend to offer here is not an elucidation but a polemical aside, sparked by some disagreement.

*   *   *   *   *

A. A. Parker, the most influential of Calderón's modern critics, has approached Calderón's theater in a way that is similar to, and perhaps modeled after, T. S. Eliot's widely imitated critical practice. Eliot and Parker value conceptual clarity in art. This taste led Eliot to regard Dante as the greatest of poets. Parker, for reasons that are moral and intellectual (not sensual), would place Calderón, too, at the summit of Parnassus. Calderón, and Dante, may belong there, but if they do it is not because their art embraces a conceptually clear vision of heaven and earth. Art does not live entirely in ideas, nor in lucidity, nor in metaphysics; it lives also in its own surface. Calderón's clarity itself is debatable, but Parker makes a good case for it in his critical essays. Take, for example, this excerpt from Parker's essay comparing Calderón's *La cisma de Inglaterra* with Shakespeare's and Fletcher's *Henry VIII*, an essay in which Parker reaches the conclusion that Calderón's is the better play:

> In *La cisma de Inglaterra* the theme of Henry VIII's divorce is . . . transformed into a significant and deeply impressive dramatic action. Since it has what *Henry VIII* has not—a powerful dramatic idea unifying the action with intricate subtlety into an admirable coherence, and leading to an inevitable conclusion—we are surely compelled to admit that the "wide difference" revealed by a comparison of the

1. This designation was coined by the British Hispanicist R. D. F. Pring-Mill in an article entitled "Los calderonistas de habla inglesa y *La vida es sueño*: métodos del análisis temático-estructural." Pring-Mill's discussion of the English Calderonians, which is complete, sympathetic, and not uncritical, confirms my predisposition to do nothing of the sort here. The reader who is really interested in English criticism of Calderón is urged to consult Pring-Mill's article.

two plays is not what Ticknor imagined it to be. The superiority of Calderón's play in conception and construction is overwhelming.[2]

Anticipating the reader's surprise at this statement, Parker adds, in a footnote:

In other respects, of course, Calderón has not the advantage. There is not the same vitality and warmth in the verse; the characters are not as natural and lifelike, and do not therefore play as readily on our emotions. But the nineteenth century standards of realism and the "poetic" are not only irrelevant to Calderón, they obscure his purpose and have actually misrepresented his extraordinary achievement. His aim is not to approximate as closely as possible to actual life, but to create self-consistent works of art, for which, in Mr. T. S. Eliot's words, "an abstraction from actual life is a necessary condition." This is not the place to discuss the formalism of Calderón's art, which would be a vast undertaking; but it may be pointed out that a relevant approach is through the principles stated in Mr. Eliot's essay, "Four Elizabethan Dramatists" in Selected Essays. Henry VIII, when compared with La Cisma, perhaps bears out his contention that "the weakness of the Elizabethan drama is not its defect in realism, but its attempt at realism," and that "the art of the Elizabethans is an impure art."[3]

One should resist the contention that Calderón, in La cisma or in any other play, is "clear" in any but the most syllogistic way. His very "coherence" is an attitude that alters reality and should be seen, if it is to be appreciated, as a reactionary and quite vulnerable response to nature's transformations. Those nineteenth-century critics who, unlike Parker, preferred their own (and Shakespeare's and Lope's) perceptions of nature to anyone's "admirable coherence" or "self-consistence," were

2. Alexander A. Parker, "Henry VIII in Shakespeare and Calderón. An Appreciation of La cisma de Ingalaterra," p. 350. Professor Parker has told me that this paper, written more than thirty years ago, no longer represents his judgment of the play and that he would now phrase differently some of the statements in the passage I quote here. I am using this article, and arguing with it, because when it appeared it was, and it still is, enormously influential.

3. Ibid.

equipped to see Calderón's distortions, although their tastes sometimes inhibited their enjoyment.

Some of the nineteenth-century critics to whom Parker refers may occasionally have demanded of art such naively "realistic" trappings as photographic fidelity, lifelike characterization, and historical accuracy; but to say that these were their main considerations is to do an injustice to them and to the writers they revered. What they argued, I think, was that a dramatic art should imitate by analogy some human action and should be faithful to what Shelley called "the truth of human passion," not to a rigid casuistry. I think that these precepts are valid ones. I think that Calderón's Scholasticism is not always natural; hence, like Shelley and Lewes and Menéndez Pelayo, I do not care for the "conceptual clarity" that Parker prizes so highly. But I think nonetheless that Calderón often transcends his own conceptual presuppositions to create an art that is personal and imaginative, an art with tensions and interests that arise from the clash that occurs when clear and orderly concepts meet and try unsuccessfully to contain a human vitality that Calderón perceives too well to ignore or suppress. Further, Calderón's art shows that attempts at suppression coincide with, and generate attempts at, rebellion. It is, finally, the will to control, an artistic effort to contain, that is the significant human characteristic of Calderón's art.

In his discussion of *La cisma de Ingalaterra* Parker asks a rhetorical question:

> Is it being false to history to view Henry VIII and all the other actors in his drama as symbols of tragic humanity, falling under the weight of unbearable responsibilities, confused by the conflict of passion and reason, blinded by pride, ambition or a self-righteous over-confidence, all erring in the darkness that is human life?[4]

This question assumes that the reader's response will be negative, but a proper (not just perverse) answer is: yes, it is false both to history and to poetry to view Henry VIII or anyone else as an illustrative symbol of any general idea, Christian or otherwise. Parker does not think so; in fact he thinks that Calderón's moral and intellectual constructs are both Christian

4. Ibid., p. 351.

and true, as he says when he compares *La cisma*'s Christian message with that of Shakespeare's and Fletcher's *Henry VIII* as it is seen by Wilson Knight. Parker writes:

> Whatever Christian sentiments are voiced by Katharine and others, [*Henry VIII*] as a whole is as non-Christian in spirit as Mr. Wilson Knight's summing-up is in statement. [Calderón's] presentation of men as imperfect beings vitally in need of redemption—doomed to either absolute or partial failure through the blindness of their intellects or the corruption of their wills; either swept away by disaster or struggling as best they can towards the dawn, but never able to gaze at the sun—is not only more consonant with Christian teaching, but surely also a more valuable, because truer, interpretation of human history.[5]

Against this conception of what is Christian and what is not, one could argue that Calderón's service to real spiritual processes and values is inhibited by his tendency to reduce values to fixed symbols, processes to manipulations. It would probably be naive to argue that Calderón's stage world is unrecognizable as a depiction of human reality. Anyone's private world, or any group's public world, may be unbalanced in Calderonian ways. Nevertheless, Calderón's own obsession with order and his fear of the instinctual are the preconditions of his dramatic world; insofar as these preconditions (however universal or faithful to human reality they may be) are conducive to the depiction of what Parker calls human tragedy, Calderón's theater is faithful to the human condition. But the truth of Calderón's vision is (as Lewes and Menéndez Pelayo maintained) closer to the relative truth that makes itself known when a rigid consciousness confronts a mutable reality than it is to nature's truth itself, which is neither static nor preformed into abstract categories. However, I would add that it seems that Calderón himself is aware, on a creative level, that the efficacy of the very principles of order that he finally embraces and upholds may be limited. In the end, they are all he has, but he does have the courage to pursue their consequences.

Parker has argued that in Calderón's honor plays the guard-

5. Ibid., p. 352.

the "inhuman" laws of honor, the murderers of wives and the monarchs who approve of such vengeance, are punished for their allegiance to the false doctrine of honor to the degree that they are frustrated, at the plays' ends, by their conditions of despondency or wifelessness. There is truth in this observation, and the moral that Parker draws from these plays (*La devoción de la cruz, El médico de su honra,* and others like them) is one that might be drawn by any reader who is, as any reader should be, appalled by what goes on within them. Parker, though, attributes his own morality to Calderón, which is a mistake. To Calderón, these husbands are victims, sufferers for the truth of a necessity that Calderón may not like but does not dismiss with a moralistic condemnation: the necessity to maintain the integrity, in fact and in appearance, of a familial and social order that represents a shaky but indispensable provision against the effects of a human will to disorder. That Calderón, and his characters, could construe and construct their choices in such self-destructive terms is a fact that anyone might attribute (as did Lewes and Menéndez Pelayo) to the mores of a society held in the thrall of a false consciousness. But if one regards Calderón as an outraged critic of this consciousness and deduces this from the existence of horror and frustration within Calderón's plays, he indulges, I think, in a kind of critical wishful thinking.

Many other critics, who in one way or another have been influenced by the work of A. A. Parker, have turned out sensitive readings of Calderón's plays. Sometimes, however, their arguments are slightly irrelevant, deranged, I think, by their following Parker in demonstrating that Calderón involved himself creatively in a condemnation of the Spanish code of honor. A. I. Watson, for example, in a subtle, thorough article on the mythological extravaganza *Los tres mayores prodigios,*[6] needlessly directs his reading of the third act toward making a point about Calderón and honor—the wrong point, I think.[7] Honor, in *Los tres mayores prodigios,* is less important dramatically as a system of values, good or bad (although Cal-

6. Pedro Calderón de la Barca, *Los tres mayores prodigios,* in *Obras completas,* 5th ed., vol. 1, ed. A. Valbuena Briones (Madrid: Aguilar, 1966), p. 1548.

7. See A. Irvine Watson, "Hercules and the Tunic of Shame: Calderón's *Los tres mayores prodigios.*"

derón's characters usually think of honor obligations as oppressive), than as a conventional engine of fate, driving a situation in which people must deal with a force they cannot control. In *Los tres mayores prodigios* the honor emotion, the concern for reputation, becomes confused and enriched with those other things—sexual jealousy, passion, death—that Calderón really seems to care about.

Calderón designed the three acts of *Los tres mayores prodigios* to be performed consecutively by three theatrical companies upon three stages. Acts 1 and 2, which dramatize versions of the stories of Jason and the Golden Fleece and of Theseus and the Minotaur, were played on stages to the right and to the left of a center stage upon which act 3, a Hercules story, was enacted as a climax, the most prodigious of the three events. Here the audience sees Hercules, the world's strongest man, beset by humiliating confusion and jealousy, as he dies by self-immolation, followed into the pyre by his wife. Watson argues that in spite of, or beneath, the play's spectacular format and rhetoric there is a treatment of a serious moral theme: the theme of marital honor. He supports his argument upon an event in act 3: Hercules, upon recapturing his innocent wife, Deianira, from an amorous centaur, Nessus, who has abducted her, still fears public opinion so much that he would prefer to leave her, alive and unnoticed, in the Mount Oeta region, rather than live with her, dishonored, he thinks, in society. Later it turns out that society takes her innocence for granted and appears to be indifferent to the issue of her honor. Hercules, however, goes through agonies of embarrassment. Thus, Watson writes, Hercules "stands revealed in his true colors: he is the slave of *Fama*—a moral coward lacking the strength to defy a society which subscribes to an unjust, inhuman code of behavior."[8]

However, I think Calderón is not an individualist in the English sense. And Hercules has more true colors than Watson reveals. Hercules' death, brought on through the agony he feels at wearing the dead centaur's tunic, is not symbolic just of "shame" (fear of public opinion) as Watson contends. It also encompasses, more or less symbolically, the private emotion of jealousy, as Hercules absorbs the killing arrow's poison, which had permeated the tunic. Furthermore, the tunic had

8. Ibid., p. 779.

been "hechizado," imbued with the power of love, as Nessus says to Deianira in his gallant dying monologue; so it appears that Eros is really behind all this turmoil. As in Calderón's other honor plays, there is a playing out of the passionate and the irrational, a demonstration of the power of sexual license to bring everyone along with it as it runs toward death. Calderón delivers this sensationally; his play has the excitement of great melodrama without being, as Watson contends, moralistic. *Los tres mayores prodigios* has the amoral grandeur that both fascinates and shocks and that is most typically, and wonderfully, Calderonian.

Appendix

Entries in the Appendix are listed according to the number of the footnote indicator that immediately follows each † symbol.

Chapter 1.

Note 1.

> I do not know the nature of my pain,
> for if I knew, what now is melancholy
> would be mere sadness. I only know
> that I can feel; what I can feel I do not know,
> since it is an illusion of the soul.

Note 4.

> Tell me, on your life, is there anyone
> who does not know that I,
> although of stainless lineage,
> am a plain and simple man?

Note 6.

> A Voice: What is this life's greatest glory?
> Chorus: Love, love.
> A Voice: There is no being on whom love's fire
> does not imprint its flame; it lives
> where man loves, animates him. Love
> loves but things that know of life,
> the tree, the flower, the bird; and so
> the greatest glory of this life is . . .
> Chorus: Love, love.

Chapter 2.

Note 3.

> The Understanding: How like the Human Senses
> have you shown yourself to be,
> in looking for the object

most responsive to your needs!
Hadn't you better emulate
the rustic Theban, whose
true penitence could mock the power
of the most peopled courts, because
it is so certain that
without pain in this life
there is no pleasure in the next?

Everyman: And how like the Understanding
have you spoken up yourself,
prescribing torment to my Senses!
Don't you see that they are human,
and ultimately they require
blandishments to turn them from
the troubles into which they're born?

Note 4.

because I know that when he sins
a man becomes a beast.

Note 5.

Everyman: Wise Understanding, I can see
that I am in great danger. I
desire to set my own desires free,
and so to live, for I could never
leave this place without companions
that my very nature gave to me.
And given that my senses, all of them,
are lost in this morass of Guilt,
I must go in to rescue them.
I know that I'll come out all right
if I go in with you.

Note 6.

(singing with recorder music)

Musicians: Now that he confesses guilt
and asks to be forgiven,
oh Penitence, you are the Rainbow,
come flying to favor him.

Note 8.

> Guilt: From the flowers I will read
> rare mysteries of Nature's books.
> At all hours you will hear
> sweet music, soft songs of the birds,
> sweet manmade verses. You'll be served
> the best of foods, prepared to tempt
> both taste and smell. To entertain
> your vision there will be those gardens
> which are our paradise,
> filled with various delights . . .
> . . . And most of all you'll have from me
> gifts from my breast, my arms' caress,
> the flattery of my affect,
> all refinements of my love,
> the truth of my desire, and the
> attention of my will, the dedication
> of my life, and finally, delights
> and tastes, gifts, pleasures, blisses,
> favors, music, dancing, games.

Note 11.

> Peasant: . . . because You know, and it is clear,
> for there's nothing You don't know,
> what part You're going to give to me,
> I'll blame myself and not the role
> if I should misinterpret it.

Note 12.

> Author: For that purpose, I will give
> to all of you, the rich and poor,
> the precepts of my Law, to mend
> the errant, teach the ignorant.
> It will tell you all what you
> must do, so that you won't complain of me.
> You have your wills; the stage is set,
> so you and you, go out and take
> the measure of life's distances.

Note 13.

> Poor Man: Why must I enact the part
> of the poor man in this play?
> Must it be a tragedy
> to me and not the others?
> When your Hand gave me this role,
> did It not also give a soul
> that's equal to a king's?
> An equal sense? An equal being?
> Why then such an unequal part?

Note 14.

> Let us eat today, and drink
> for tomorrow we shall die.

Note 15.

> I know it is God's wish that we,
> in measuring the immensity
> of His love, His knowledge and His power,
> should take advantage of the arts
> which, when applied in human ways,
> can be examples to us.
> Since the finite cannot understand
> the infinite, there has to be
> a visible medium there to help
> us understand, with our small means,
> as an imagined concept passes
> into practical conceit.
> Let's see to it that this is shown
> in the theaters of our time

Note 16.

> Oh me! I fall enveloped in fire,
> dragging my shadow to a place
> where I can't see myself! Hard rocks
> will here inter my entrails
> in dark chambers.

Chapter 3.

Note 2.

> I rise to such an angry pitch,
> an Etna urging to erupt,
> I'll rip apart my chest
> to tear out pieces of my heart

Note 3.

> Heaven, how well it serves your ends
> to keep me as a slave.
> With freedom I would be a giant.
> On stone foundations I would build
> mountains of jasper, climbing to burst
> the crystal windows of the sun.

Note 4.

> I know that I am composed of both man and beast.

Note 5.

> Heaven, I demand to know,
> since you punish me this way,
> how my birth could be a sin
> that so offends you;

Note 6.

> It may be an error to believe
> too easily in portents, for
> although their tendency may be
> to lead him into danger,
> perhaps he will not be subdued,
> because the most unhappy fate,
> the most violent inclination,
> the most unforgiving planet
> only can incline the will;
> they cannot force it.

Note 7.

What is life? A frenzy.
What is life? An illusion.
A shadow, a fiction.
And the greatest good is small
for all life is a dream
and dreams themselves are but dreams.

Note 11.

the timorous light which the day still holds

Note 12.

Heaven, show me a path, although
I doubt that there's a way through this abyss
where all the sky is portent,
all the earth a prodigy.

Note 13.

an asp of metal which will spit
the penetrating venom of two bullets,
whose fire will scandalize the air.

Note 14.

The bird is born, and scarcely
does it don its glittered cloak,
a feathered flower, winged bouquet

Note 15.

Who, to secure an earthly glory,
would give up a divine one?

Note 18.

I only loved a woman . . .
And it truly happened, I believe,
for everything has vanished,
and this remains.

Note 19.

> Why should you be so amazed,
> if my teacher was a dream
> and I'm afraid and anxious, lest
> I should awake to find myself
> again in prison? Even if
> this should not be, just to dream it
> is enough, for that was how
> I learned that human happiness
> passes, finally, like a dream,
> and I must take advantage of
> the time that's left

Chapter 4.

Note 4.

> To the weight of the years
> the eminent must surrender;
> for the easy hand of time
> no conquest can be difficult.

Note 5.

> Fernando: Enrique, you must lose your fear of all such things.
> Your falling now was nothing more
> than the very earth's request
> for your arms' lordly welcome.

Note 9.

> What purpose has this beauty,
> as long as it is mine,
> when I have no pleasure,
> when I have no joy.

Note 10.

> Could it have pleased her to hear music
> whose instruments are the chains and irons
> that imprison us?

Note 11.

> I only know that I can feel;
> What I can feel I do not know,
> since it is an illusion of the soul.

Note 13.

> to die as good men die,
> with steadfast souls

Note 14.

> Fernando: Oh, if my voice could only move
> someone to pity me,
> that I might live my suffering
> for even an instant more!

Note 18.

> If Fénix is what pains him, I will not compete for her.

Note 19.

> Fénix: The ransom for a corpse! Whoever
> knew such pain? There can be no joy
> for an unhappy woman.
> In the end a corpse will own me?
> Who will this dead man be?

Note 22.

> Fénix: Oh heaven, what is this I see?
> Fernando: What do you marvel at?
> Fénix: I marvel at both hearing you and
> seeing you.
> Fernando: No need to swear it.
> I believe you. Fénix, I
> who wish to serve you
> have brought flowers, hieroglyphs
> of what my fate will bring. At dawn
> they were born, with the day
> they died.
> Fénix: That flower,
> when it was discovered, was called the *maravilla*.

Fernando: Tell me what flower is not a "marvel"
          when I give it to you.
Fénix: That's true.
          What caused your new estate?
Fernando: My fate.
Fénix: So rigorous it is?
Fernando: So strong.
Fénix: It grieves me.
Fernando: Well, don't be alarmed.
Fénix: Why not?
Fernando: Because mankind is born
          subject to fortune and death.
Fénix: Are you
          Fernando?
Fernando: Yes, I am.

Note 23.

Fernando: These, that were all pomp and were all glory
          when in the morning's dawning light they awoke,
          will be before the dark but vain and pitiable,
          sleeping in the cold arms of the night.
          This hue, which challenges the heavens,
          a rainbow striped in scarlet, snow, and gold,
          will be a warning to mankind's endeavors:
          so much attempted in a day so short!
          The roses rose at dawn to make their flowers,
          and in their flourishing they but grew old:
          cradle and sepulchre in a bud together.
          And so do men their enterprise behold,
          born in a day, in that day to expire;
          when centuries have passed, they were but hours.

Note 24.

You have given me horror and fear

Note 25.

Fénix: Those features of the light, those scintillations
       which with superior threats take of the Sun
       their food from its resplendent emanations,
       that they might live like it, but at the cost of pain,

are all nocturnal flowers, but so fair
that in ephemera they burn their loves;
for if a day is century to the flowers,
one night is an eternity to the stars.
Then from this fugitive Spring a human fortune,
now favorable, now not, can be inferred:
it is our register, no matter what the Sun does.
What term of life is there for man to hope for,
what change is there to be which is not given
by a star, that's born and dies with every night?

Note 26.

D. Alfonso: King of Fez, to keep you from
the thought that Fernando dead is worth
less than is this beauty, I will trade
her for him as he lies there.
Send me the snow to be exchanged
for crystal, January for the days of May,
roses for diamonds,
and, in short, an unhappy corpse
for a divine image.

Chapter 5.

Note 3.

Don Manuel: My misfortunes are like hydras
born again from their cold ash.
What shall I do in this blind abyss,
a human labyrinth to me?
She is the sister of Don Luis,
when I thought her a free woman.
If he felt my offense to his taste,
how will he feel about his honor?
What an unjust torment! She is his sister:
If I try to free her, defend her with my blood,
entrusting her excusing to my steel,
my guilt is even greater, since it is
as much as saying that I've been
a traitor to her house. To try

to exculpate myself by blaming her
is to say that she's at fault, and that
my honor will not let me do.
What can I do? If I defend her
I'm a traitor; if I leave her
I'm a wretch; if I protect her,
a bad guest; inhuman if I give her over
to her brother. I'm a bad friend
if I keep her; ungrateful, if I free her,
for their noble treatment,
ungrateful, if I don't, for her noble love.
Well, in any case
this will be bad for me; I'll die fighting.
Don't worry, my lady; (*to Doña Ángela*)
I am a nobleman, and you're with me now.

Chapter 6.

Note 7.

Doña Mencía: I saw them from the tower,
and although I can't distinguish
who they are, Jacinta, I can tell
that a disaster has occurred.
A brave knight came, on so swift a brute
that in the wind he seemed a bird
in flight; and there is reason to presume it,
for a tuft of feathers tinged the air.
Field and sun competed
in lending him their splendor.
The fields gave up their flowers;
the sun bestowed its stars;
and they traded off in such a way,
and in such a way they shone,
that they seemed all like the sun
and like the Spring in everything.
The horse, then, raced and fell;
what was a bird became a rose,
and when it spilled to earth it reproduced
the luster of sun, sky, earth, wind,
bird, brute, and star and flower.

Note 8.

>   Enrique: Oh, Don Arias, the fall
>   was not by chance, but an omen
>   of my death! [*To Mencía*] And rightly so,
>   for it was divine decree
>   that I die here, feeling this way,
>   where you are married.
>   We can have at once
>   condolence and congratulation
>   for your wedding and my burial.

Note 9.

>   Mencía: . . . I'm only glad
>   at having now to feel,
>   and having desires to conquer,
>   for there is no virtue
>   without experience

Note 10.

>   If your love does not incline
>   to a correction, if you'll not
>   leave behind your vain designs
>   on beauty that is not for you,
>   but of a place where a vassal's soul
>   rules with sovereign law, perhaps
>   I will invoke my justice,
>   from which my own blood is not exempt.

Note 12.

>   Gutierre: . . . Did I say jealousy? Jealousy?
>   Well, enough of that, for when
>   a husband starts to know
>   that he is jealous, reason is gone,
>   and it is the scientific cure
>   that the surgeon of his honor wants.

Note 13.

>   Gutierre: Jealous! What do you know of jealousy?
>   I myself know nothing, but if I did . . .

Mencía (aside): Oh!
    Gutierre: ... feel ... What is jealousy?
              Atoms, illusions, and unrest, why if
              of even a slave, a servant, I
              should have the shadow of a doubt,
              I would, in public, tear pieces of
              her heart out of her body, and then,
              enveloped in blood, released in fire,
              I'd eat her heart
              in mouthfuls, drink her blood,
              extract her soul, and shatter it,
              if her soul could feel the pain!
              But why am I speaking in this way?
    Mencía: You fill my soul with terror!
    Gutierre: Oh God! My wife, my glory
              and my love, Mencía, pardon me
              (by your eyes) for this wild raging.
              A projection of my mind
              carried my thought away.
              Go in, for Heaven's sake, I promise
              that I look on you with deference
              and respect. I am ashamed
              of this excess; I left my senses.
              I was not myself.
Mencía (aside): This horror, fear and dread
              are paroxysms of my death.
Gutierre (aside): I am the surgeon of my honor;
              I'll cover my disgrace with earth.

Note 15.

    Gutierre: If I should see myself again
              in such an unhappy quandary,
              as when I found your brother, masked
              and in my house . . . ?
       King: Do not give credit to suspicions.
    Gutierre: And if, perhaps, behind my bed
              I find, my lord, Enrique's dagger?
       King: Presume that in this world there are

a thousand bribe-corrupted servants,
and rely upon your prudence.
Gutierre: Sometimes, my lord, it's not enough.
What if I see him, night and day,
hovering around my house?
King: Complain to me.
Gutierre: And what if I should,
in doing so, hear something worse
than I suspected?
King: What does it matter,
if he's discouraged; her beauty defies him
as a rampart does the wind.
Gutierre: And if, returning to my house,
I find a letter to the prince
that begs him to stay on?
King: For everything there is a remedy.
Gutierre: But is there one for that?
King: Yes, Gutierre.
Gutierre: What, my lord?
King: Your own.
Gutierre: What is it?
King: Bleeding.

Note 16.

Gutierre: . . . Now look this way. You'll see the sun
all bloody, and the moon eclipsed,
the stars extinguished, spheres erased.
You'll see the saddest, most unlucky
beauty, who gave me a death
far worse than hers, when she
left me with my soul.

Chapter 7.

Note 3.

Isabel (aside): Oh, stars above,
This is much concern,
or else it's caution.

Note 4.

> The flowers of the rosemary,
> my darling Isabel,
> are blue today: tomorrow
> they'll be honey.

Note 5.

> Casilda: . . . When the meal is done,
>   we fold our hands
>   in thanks for the mercy God has shown.
>   We go to bed;
>   it pains the dawn
>   to call us when the hour has come.

Note 6.

>   this afternoon
> I went to see the fields, the stacks
> of grain are so impressive
> in their richness, that they seem
> like mountains of gold, and yet more precious
> for the setting lent them by the sky.
> The fork, allowing a soft breeze
> to wound them gently, left the grains
> on this side, chaff on that—for even
> here the meek give way before
> the strong. I pray God grant me leave
> to store it in the granary
> before a squall blows it away
> or a wind lays it to waste!

Chapter 8.

Note 3.

> You are with child. You will give birth
> to a beautiful boy. A voice, and a
> great beauty will both seek his end
> in love and hate. Protect him from
> all that he sees and hears.

Note 4.

For when I tried, mad with desire,
to grasp it (Can such pain exist?)
I clouded its celestial light;
I touch the crystal mirror alone,
and not the crystal's soul.

Chapter 9.

Note 1.

A brave knight came on so light a brute
that in the wind he seemed a bird in flight;
and there's reason to presume it,
for a tuft of feathers tinged the air.
The fields and Sun competed
in giving him their splendor;
the fields gave up their flowers;
the Sun bestowed its stars;
and they traded off in such a way
and in such a way they shone
that they seemed all like the Sun
and like the Spring in everything.
The horse, then, ran, and tripped;
what was a bird became a rose
and when it fell to earth it showed
the luster of Sun, sky, earth, wind
bird, brute, and star and flower.

Note 2.

I have yet to know a limit
to the joy of meeting you.
What I heard was little
when compared to what I see.
Your speech, your acts, my son and lord,
fit you so well that they proclaim
the soul within your breast to be
a great one. How fortunate
to lose my way, for then I met
you sooner through an error well-conceived.

As the tempest in an angry sea,
when it subsides, admits once more
the starlight, so my error
was the night, this river the sea,
my coach the ship, and I
the pilot, you my star.

Note 3.

All that lives is born of love
and of love is sustained.
And all that dies, it is a cruelty
that does unmake our lives.

Note 5.

The miracle of your beauty
I presumed to be the kind event
of my new life, but now I think,
in disillusion, that it was
the vengeance of my death, because
it's certain that I'm dying, and
there are no miracles
to be examined in death.

Bibliography

Books

Casalduero, Joaquín. *Estudios sobre el teatro español: Lope de Vega, Guillén de Castro, Cervantes, Tirso de Molina, Ruiz de Alarcón, Calderón, Moratín, Duque de Rivas.* Madrid: Editorial Gredos, 1962.

Castro, Américo. *De la edad conflictiva: el drama de la honra en España y en su literatura.* 2d ed. Madrid: Taurus, 1961.

————. *Hacia Cervantes.* 3d ed. rev. Madrid: Taurus, 1967.

————. *La realidad histórica de España.* 2d ed. Mexico: Editorial Porrúa, 1962.

Constandse, A. L. *Le Baroque Espagnole et Calderón de la Barca.* Amsterdam: Boekhandel "Plus Ultra," 1951.

de Madariaga, Salvador. *Shelley and Calderón and Other Essays on English and Spanish poetry.* Port Washington, N.Y.: Kennikat Press, 1965.

Farinelli, Arturo. *La vita è un sogno.* 2 vols. Torino: Fratelli Bocca, 1916.

Frutos Cortés, Eugenio. *Calderón de la Barca.* Barcelona: Editorial Labor, 1949.

Honig, Edwin. *Calderón and the Seizures of Honor.* Cambridge, Mass.: Harvard University Press, 1972.

Kossoff, A. David, and Amor y Vásquez, José, eds. *Homenaje a William L. Fichter.* Madrid: Castalia, 1971.

Lewes, George Henry. *The Spanish Drama: Lope de Vega and Calderón.* London: Charles Knight, 1846.

Menéndez y Pelayo, Marcelino. *Calderón y su teatro: conferencias dadas en el círculo de la Unión Católica.* 3d ed. Madrid: A. Pérez Dubrull, 1884.

Parker, Alexander A. *The Allegorical Drama of Calderón: An Introduction to the Autos Sacramentales.* Oxford: The Dolphin Book Co., 1943.

Sauvage, Micheline. *Calderón, dramaturge.* Paris: L'Arche, 1959.

Schlegel, August Wilhelm. *A Course of Lectures on Dramatic Art and Literature.* Translated by John Black. London: H. G. Bohn, 1846.

Sloman, Albert E. *The Dramatic Craftsmanship of Calderón.* Oxford: The Dolphin Book Co., 1958.

————. *The Sources of Calderón's "El príncipe constante."* Oxford: Blackwell, 1950.

Trench, R. C. *Calderón, his Life and Genius*. New York: Redfield, 1856.

Valbuena Prat, Ángel. *Calderón, su personalidad, su arte, su estilo y sus obras*. Barcelona: Editorial Juventud, 1941.

———. *Historia del teatro español*. Barcelona: Noguer, 1956.

Vossler, Karl. *Lope de Vega y su tiempo*. Translated by Ramón Gómez de la Serna. Madrid: Revista de Occidente, 1933.

Wardropper, Bruce W., et al. *Critical Essays on the Theatre of Calderón*. New York: New York University Press, 1965.

Wilson, Edward M. *Poesías líricas en las obras dramáticas de Calderón*. London: Tamesis Books, 1964.

Articles

Bataillon, Marcel. "Essai d'explication de l'*auto sacramental*." *Bulletin Hispanique* 42 (1940): 193–212.

Casa, Frank P. "Crime and Responsibility in *El médico de su honra*." In *Homenaje a William L. Fichter*, edited by A. David Kosoff and José Amor y Vásquez, pp. 127–37. Madrid: Castalia, 1971.

Castro, Américo. "Algunas observaciones acerca del concepto del honor en los siglos XVI y XVII." *Revista de Filología Española* 3 (1916): 1–50.

Cirot, G. "El gran teatro del mundo." *Bulletin Hispanique* 43 (1941): 290–305.

Dunn, Peter N. "Honour and the Christian background in Calderón." *Bulletin of Hispanic Studies* 37 (1960): 75–105.

———. "The horoscope motif in *La vida es sueño*." *Atlante* 1 (1953): 187–201.

Entwistle, W. J. "Justina's Temptation: An Approach to the Understanding of Calderón." *Modern Language Review* 40 (1945): 180–89.

Gates, Eunice J. "Góngora and Calderón." *Hispanic Review* 5 (1937): 241–58.

Gilman, Stephen. "The 'Comedia' in the Light of the New Criticism." *Bulletin of the Comediantes*, 1960.

Hesse. Everett W. "Obsesiones en *El mayor monstruo del mundo* de Calderón." *Estudios* 8 (1952): 395–409.

Honig, Edwin. "The Seizures of Honor in Calderón." *Kenyon Review* 23 (1961): 426–47.

Jones, C. A. "Honor in *El alcalde de Zalamea*." *Modern Language Review* 50 (1955): 444–49.

————. "*Honor* in Spanish Golden Age Drama: Its Relation to Real Life and to Morals." *Bulletin of Hispanic Studies* 35 (1958): 199–201.

King, Willard F. Introduction to *The Knight of Olmedo* (*El Caballero de Olmedo*). Lincoln: University of Nebraska Press, 1972.

Parker, Alexander A. "Henry VIII in Shakespeare and Calderón: An Appreciation of *La cisma de Ingalaterra*." *Modern Language Review* 43 (1948): 327–52.

————. "The Theology of the Devil in the Drama of Calderón." The Aquinas Society of London: Aquinas Paper no. 32. London, 1958.

————. "Towards a Definition of Calderonian Tragedy." *Bulletin of Hispanic Studies* 39 (1962): 223–37.

Pring-Mill, R. D. F. "Los calderonistas de habla inglesa y *La vida es sueño*: métodos del análisis temático-estructural." In *Litterae Hispanae et Lusitanae*, edited by Hans Flasche, pp. 369–414. Munich: Max Hueber Verlag, 1968.

Reichenberger, Arnold G. "Calderón's *El príncipe constante*, a Tragedy?" *Modern Language Notes* 75 (1960): 668–70.

————. "The Uniqueness of the Comedia." *Hispanic Review* 28 (1950): 303–16.

Reyes, Alfonso. "Un tema de *La vida es sueño*: el hombre y la naturaleza en el monólogo de Segismundo. *Revista de Filología Española* 4 (1917): 1–25, 237–76.

Sciacca, M. F. "Vida y sueño en *La vida es sueño* de Calderón." *Clavileño* 1 (1950): 1–9.

Sloman, Albert E. "The Structure of Calderón's *La vida es sueño*." *Modern Language Review* 48 (1953): 293–300.

Soons, Alan. "The Convergence of Doctrine and Symbol in *El médico de su honra*." *Romanische Forschungen* 72 (1960): 370–80.

Spitzer, Leo. "A Central Theme and its Structural Equivalent in Lope's *Fuente Ovejuna*." *Hispanic Review* 23 (1955): 274–92.

————. "Classical and Christian Ideas of World Harmony." *Traditio* 2 (1944): 409–64; 3 (1945): 307–64.

————. "Die Figur der Fénix in Calderón's *Standhaften Prinzen*." *Romanische Jahrbuch* 10 (1959): 305–35. Translated and reprinted in *Critical Essays on the Theatre of Calderón*, edited by Bruce W. Wardropper, pp. 137–60. New York: New York University Press, 1965.

Valbuena Prat, Ángel. "Los autos sacramentales de Calderón: clasificación y análisis." *Revue Hispanique* 61 (1924): 1–302.

Wardropper, Bruce W. "Poetry and Drama in Calderón's *El médico de su honra.*" *Romanic Review* 59 (1958): 3–11.

Watson, A. Irvine. "Hercules and the Tunic of Shame: Calderón's *Los tres mayores prodigios.*" In *Homenaje a William L. Fichter,* edited by A. David Kossoff and José Amor y Vásquez, pp. 773–83. Madrid: Castalia, 1971.

––––––. "*El pintor de su deshonra* and the Neo-Aristotelian Theory of Tragedy." *Bulletin of Hispanic Studies* 40 (1963): 17–34.

Whitby, William M. "Rosaura's Role in the Structure of *La vida es sueño.*" *Hispanic Review* 28 (1960): 16–27.

Wilhelm, J. "La crítica Calderoniana en los siglos XIX y XX en Alemania." *Cuadernos Hispano-Americanos* 73 (1956): 47–56.

Wilson, Edward M. "The Four Elements in the Imagery of Calderón." *Modern Language Review* 31 (1936): 34–47.

––––––. "Gerald Brenan's Calderón." *Bulletin of the Comediantes* 6, no. 1 (1952).

––––––. "*La vida es sueño.*" *Revista de la Universidad de Buenos Aires* 3–4 (1946): 61–78.

Wilson, Edward M., and Entwistle, W. J. "Calderón's *Príncipe constante*: Two Appreciations." *Modern Language Review* 34 (1939): 207–22.

Index

A

Autos sacramentales, 7, 14, 18–28, 36, 43, 46

B

"British school" of Calderón criticism, 9,
63–64, 98–105
Burke, Kenneth, 17

C

Calderón de la Barca, Pedro: aesthetic
organization of plays, 11, 26–27, 32,
99–102; and Eros, 9, 10, 40–41, 50–51, 55,
59, 68, 76, 81, 104–5; relation to honor values,
9, 16, 57–61, 64–66, 75–76, 80–81, 103; as
Jesuit playwright, 22; as poet, 35–36, 68,
92–97; poetry compared with Lope's, 94–97;
political values, 13, 24–28, 37–38, 78n, 84–86;
El alcalde de Zalamea, 5, 7, 16, 17, 78–86;
La cisma de Ingalaterra, 99–102; *La dama
duende,* 16, 17, 57–62; *La devoción de la
cruz,* 53, 103; *Eco y Narciso,* 17, 87–91;
Los encantos de la Culpa, 16, 18–24; *El gran
teatro del mundo,* 16, 23–28; *El mágico
prodigioso,* 10, 51; *El médico de su honra,*
16, 17, 61, 63–77, 92–94, 96–97, 103; *El
príncipe constante,* 2, 7, 14, 42, 43–56;
Los tres mayores prodigios, 103–5; *La vida
es sueño,* 13, 14, 15, 17, 26, 29–42, 44,
45–46, 54, 99n
Camus, Albert, 53, 61
Castro, Américo: on honor drama as historical
analogy, 5–8, 75; on Spanish values, 3,
13; on *La vida es sueño,* 33–34
Cervantes, Miguel de, 3, 65, 84
Clarín (Leopoldo Alas), 63
Comedia, 1–10; compared with Hollywood
Westerns, 4–5; as a social vision, 83–86

F

Farinelli, Arturo: on *La vida es sueño,* 37–38
Fergusson, Francis, 22–23
Ford, John, 4, 5
Free will, 13–15, 22, 31–34, 37, 39

DATE

DEMCO 38-297